Contextual
Architecture

Architectural Record Books

Affordable Houses

Apartments, Townhouses and Condominiums, 2/e

Architecture 1970-1980: A Decade of Change

The Architectural Record Book of Vacation Houses, 2/e

Buildings for Commerce and Industry

Buildings for the Arts

Engineering for Architecture

Great Houses for View Sites, Beach Sites, Sites in
the Woods, Meadow Sites, Small Sites, Sloping Sites,
Steep Sites and Flat Sites

Hospitals and Health Care Facilities, 2/e

Houses Architects Design for Themselves

Houses of the West

Institutional Buildings

Interior Spaces Designed by Architects

Office Building Design, 2/e

Places for People: Hotels, Motels, Restaurants, Bars,
Clubs, Community Recreation Facilities, Camps, Parks,
Plazas, Playgrounds

Public, Municipal and Community Buildings

Religious Buildings

Recycling Buildings: Renovations, Remodelings,
Restorations and Reuse

Techniques of Successful Practice, 2/e

A Treasury of Contemporary Houses

Architectural Record Series Books

Ayers: Specifications for Architecture, Engineering and Construction

Feldman: Building Design for Maintainability

Heery: Time, Cost and Architecture

Heimsath: Behavioral Architecture

Hopf: Designer's Guide to OSHA

Portman and Barnett: The Architect as Developer

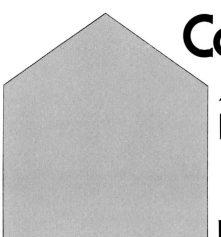

Contextual Architecture:
Responding to Existing Style

Edited by Keith Ray

An Architectural Record Book
McGraw-Hill Book Company

New York
St. Louis
San Francisco
Auckland
Bogotá
Hamburg
Johannesburg
London
Madrid
Mexico
Montreal
New Delhi
Panama
Paris
São Paulo
Singapore
Sydney
Tokyo
Toronto

The articles in this book were written by the editors of Architectural Record, most particularly Mildred F. Schmertz, William Marlin, Gerald Allen, Charles K. Hoyt, and Janet Nairn.

"Old Pavilion, Stanford University" was written by Joy Ross and the essay "Dixwell Fire Station" was contributed by Robert L. Miller.

The editors for this book were Jeremy Robinson and Patricia Markert

The designer was Irving Weksler.

The renderings featured in the introduction were drawn by Steven Bauer.

The production supervisors were Elizabeth Dineen and Paul A. Malchow.

Printed and bound by Halliday Lithograph Corporation.

Library of Congress Cataloging in Publication Data

Main entry under title:

Contextual architecture.

   "An Architectural record book."
   Includes index.
     1. Buildings—Remodeling for other use.
     2. Buildings—Repair and reconstruction.
     3. Buildings—Maintenance and repair.
     4. Architecture and history.   I.   Ray, Keith.
NA2793.C66   720'.28   80-13228
ISBN 0-07-002332-8

1234567890   HDHD   89876543210

Table of Contents

Continued

Table of Contents Continued

Introduction

Preservation, restoration, adaptive use, contextual design—all are terms very unfamiliar to architects only a few years ago. Yet suddenly, these and similar concepts have burst upon the current scene because of dramatic changes in American society in general and in architectural thought in particular. Among these societal changes are the environmental/conservation movement, the current national nostalgia, and the growing disenchantment with the sterility of suburbia and the hostility of many cities. While such forces and their sources are beyond the scope of this book, they have produced a burgeoning interest in old buildings.

This interest is primarily due to the elaborate and varied nature of historic buildings. The massing and ornamentation of their exteriors are a visual pleasure even when repeated in block upon block of rowhouses. Historic interiors often have an individuality missing in many contemporary buildings. And the ornament and details of historic buildings show human craftsmanship and care that is unaffordable today. Consequently, people are beginning to save old buildings, both individually and in whole neighborhoods.

1. The Campadoglio, Rome

To remain of service to society, these buildings often have to be modified for new uses —or new buildings have to be inserted among the existing ones to maintain the living fabric of our cities. But modification to existing buildings and new buildings cognizant of their surroundings present unfamiliar design relationships between the new and old. Contextual design, designing in relation to the context, then, is the point of this book. It elucidates the design relationship between old and new buildings by illustrating the variety of options available. This approach is not intended to address the philosophical problems of designing new buildings compatible with old ones, but instead is meant to provide a source of design ideas to help both architects and lay people solve specific design problems. Consequently, the book is divided into four chapters based on the scale of interiors, alterations, additions, and finally to the largest scale of in-fill. Within each chapter, the examples show the wide range of possibilities, extending from reproducing or reusing the old building to sympathetically contrasting with it. Those involved in contextual design problems may turn to the appropriate chapter and review a variety of possible design solutions.

An obvious first step in this analysis of design relationships is to examine architectural history, since every period has had to deal with buildings of previous periods. Not all ages viewed existing buildings with the reverence

2. The Campadoglio, Rome

4. Il Duomo, Florence

that many of today's preservationists demand. For example, consider Michelangelo's urban design masterpiece, the Campadoglio in Rome (illustration 1). He was commissioned in 1538 to remodel the Capitoline Hill area, where the medieval Palazzo dei Senatori and the 1450 Palazzo dei Conservatori were located. Michelangelo accepted the obtuse angle between the buildings and completed the space by adding the Capitoline Museum opposite the Palazzo dei Conservatori. But in a bold move, he redesigned the facades of both existing buildings. While the unity of this magnificent space would be seriously impaired without Michelangelo's consistent facades (illustration 2), imagine the furor such actions would produce today.

Besides such "insensitive" remodelings, other ages often produced juxtapositions between new and existing buildings that are as jarring as those produced today. At Kings College of Cambridge University, James Gibbs obviously felt no obligation to subordinate his 1724 Fellow's Building to the beautiful Gothic Chapel (illustration 3). Instead, he produced an excellent building in the contemporary manner. An excellent building, but contextual it is not.

3. King's College, Cambridge University

5. Santa Maria Novella, Florence

Other designers, however, were more cognizant of the surroundings. The facades of four European churches present an excellent study in contextual design because of their similar problem and diverse solutions. Preindustrial churches were often built over several generations with the facade usually completed last. At completion, the prevailing architectural style could be entirely different from that of earlier parts of the church, leaving the designer the dilemma of how to finish the church stylistically.

For the Florence cathedral, the designer chose replication. His 1887 facade is a logical extension of the earlier Gothic structure (illustration 4). Across town, Alberti was slightly less reverential in his facade for Santa

6. St. Etienne du Mont, Paris

Maria Novella. Rather than replicate, he chose to unite the contemporary idiom and the existing structure in an inventive combination of classical forms that subordinate the existing Gothic silhouette and openings (illustration 5). In Paris, the 1610 facade of S. Étienne du Mont also combines the classical and Gothic. Here, however, the product is a startling collision of the two styles (illustration 6). And finally, the 1616 Salomon de Brosse facade for S. Gervais in Paris illustrates the approach most often seen today—contrast.

The classical facade is literally applied to the Gothic building behind it (illustrations 7 & 8). While this particular example is rather abrupt, the sympathetic juxtaposition of contrasting styles can increase the appreciation for the intrinsic qualities of each style.

The above examples represent the essence of this book; that a sympathetic modification of an existing building or group of buildings can be accomplished by a variety of options, ranging from reproducing the context to sympathetically contrasting with it. Because of its organization according to these options, the book both aids understanding the problems of contextual design and provides a source of ideas for solving these problems.

7. St. Gervais, Paris

8. St. Gervais, Paris

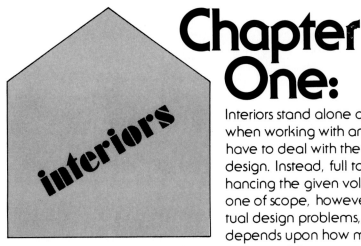

Chapter One:

interiors

Interiors stand alone as a separate category because, when working with an interior, the designer does not have to deal with the site-related demands of urban design. Instead, full talent can be concentrated on enhancing the given volume. The category is primarily one of scope, however, since, as with all other contextual design problems, the form of the enhancement depends upon how much the original interior is modified. The structural and aesthetic condition of the original interior, the future use, the budget, the designer's personal taste, and a variety of other factors determine whether the interior will be restored, have new elements added, or be replaced entirely by a new interior.

Restoration, of course, involves the least modification to the original concept of the interior. Included under the heading of restoration, however, are several important distinctions. A house museum, for instance, is generally an attempt to recreate as closely as possible the appearance of the house at a particular point in time. Two examples shown here, the Arts and Industries Building (p. 20) and the St. Louis Art Museum (p. 8), present significantly different approaches to restoration. Rather than meticulously recreating a specific point in time, the interiors evoke the image of the original architectural style. This distinction is particularly significant in the case of the Beaux Arts St. Louis Art Museum, where the original polychromatic interior was rejected in favor of a monochromatic scheme more consistent with the image of the period.

More radical than restoration is the combination of new and existing elements. New elements can be added to an existing interior in two philosophically different ways, depending upon the goal. In the less radical approach, the new elements continue the "flavor" of the existing interior in a blend that makes no clear distinction between new and old. Effect rather than exactitude is the goal. In the more radical approach, effect is achieved through exactitude. The new is carefully differentiated from the existing. Because of the inherent contrast, the differentiation heightens the appreciation of both architectural styles. This effect is clearly seen in the new work at Winchester and Norwich cathedrals (pp. 36, 37), where the elegant minimalism of contemporary glass and bronze is stunningly played against the solidity and texture of the Medieval stonework. Contrast and continuation—both are ways to add new elements to existing interiors.

The most radical approach to a building interior is to replace the old with something completely different. Again, contrast between new and old plays an important role, but here the contrast is between the historic exterior and the contemporary interior. The new interior may be installed because of the structural condition of the original, its lack of aesthetic quality, and/or the requirements of the new use. While some preservationists may lament the loss of original elements, at least the building's exterior, with all its important contributions to the street and neighborhood, is saved.

The lack of exterior design requirements separates interiors into a distinct category when discussing contextual design. Yet, as in problems of larger scope, the techniques for dealing with interiors are defined by the amount of change that will occur to the existing architecture. For interiors, the range of possibilities includes restoration, various methods of adding new elements, and the total replacement of the interior within the existing building shell. However, the following interiors illustrate that the means of executing these four different approaches are as varied as the existing buildings to which they are applied.

THE OLD
FEDERAL COURTS BUILDING

Another way that the Federal Government is trying to support the cause of architecture
is by giving its buildings away—by dramatically easing the procedures for transferring
handsome but no longer needed buildings to local authorities who promise to bring them back to life.
The Old Federal Courts Building in St. Paul, Minnesota, is one of the first in what
may become a long string of renovative successes under this plan.

In 1971 former President Nixon signed an Executive order that directed the General Services Administration to provide leadership in maintaining the historical and cultural environment in the United States. GSA, in other words, was to become a preservationist, and it was asked to begin at home by surveying its more than ten thousand buildings to single out those of special historical and architectural worth, nominating the ones it found to the National Register. Very shortly thereafter, the GSA established its Office of Fine Arts and Historic Preservation, and, most importantly, it drafted and sponsored a Surplus Property Act Amendment (Public Law 92-362), which was passed by the Congress in 1972.

This was the stitch in time for a growing and growingly frustrated band of city officials and private citizens in St. Paul, Minnesota, who had been trying for years finally to implement a plan to put the Old Federal Courts Building back to some good use. The building had been a centerpiece in the architecture of downtown St. Paul, and as downtown had decayed over the years so had the centerpiece, so that when the Federal government moved out in 1965 the Old Federal Courts Building was a sorry shadow of its former self. But if the building's decline had paralleled the decline of the downtown, why should not the reverse also be possible, with a renovation of the building serving as a symbol for the revitalization of a whole area? Besides, it was handsome, and it also contained a great deal of space that could be put to some good use.

The problem was in finding the precise use, finding the money, and—above all—finding the way to meet the government's stringent requirements for transferring the building to local hands. Until 1972, the Surplus Property Act provided that, once a building had been declared surplus, it could either be sold for its appraised price to anyone or it could be given away to some non-profit, non-revenue-producing group whose activities benefited the general public. But a further condition of this latter possibility was that the group in question would also be subject to the detailed approval of either the Department of Health, Education, and Welfare or

Shin Koyama photos

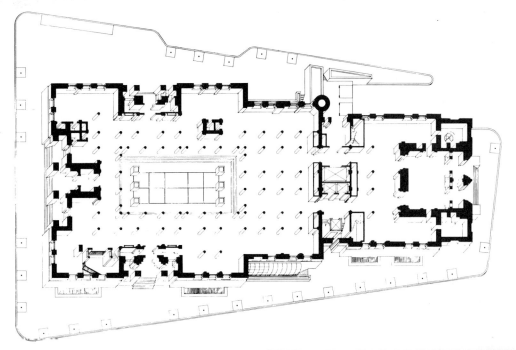

The photograph on the opposite page shows the Fifth Street elevation of the Old Federal Courts Building in St. Paul—now converted into a public cultural center and renamed "Landmark Center." A plan of the main floor of the building is shown on the right.

the Department of the Interior, depending on the nature of its activities. Enthusiasts in St. Paul for the renovation of the Old Federal Courts Building had tried without success to buy the building outright from the Federal government (noting that money paid to purchase it would reduce dangerously the coffers for its renovation), and they had also developed a number of specific proposals for uses that, it was hoped, would qualify the building for being given away outright by the government. All of these had been rejected by the bureaucracies.

The Congress (and the General Services Administration) simplified the entire process in 1972 and provided a much-needed break in the log jam. Now to be eligible for transfer, a Federal building had only to be surplus property, to be on the National Register, and to be the subject of an adequately funded plan for adaptive re-use. It could now be used for revenue-producing purposes and for a broad range of activities, as long as its status as a public historic landmark was not violated.

And so in October, 1972, the Old Federal Courts Building was turned over to the City of St. Paul for the token sum of one dollar. A principal occupant was to be the St. Paul Ramsey Arts and Science Council—a vigorous centralized administrative and fund-raising agency for most of St. Paul's and surrounding Ramsey County's artistic and scientific organizations.

The original building was designed and constructed from 1892 to 1902 by the United States Treasury Department under the architectural direction of Willoughby J. Edbrooke and James Knox Taylor. The first steps in its renovation and restoration—begun in 1973 by St. Paul architect Brooks Cavin—were the cleaning of the warm, pink St. Cloud granite of which the building is built and the replacement of the existing composition roof with one made of clay tiles from the original molds rediscovered in Ohio. At this time three of the original courtrooms were partially restored for public meetings and recitals.

While this was happening, an initial programming study and a preliminary budget were also being prepared by the firm of

Dober Associates in Cambridge, Massachusetts. In 1974, the firms of Perry, Dean, Stahl & Rogers, in Boston, and Winsor/Faricy, in St. Paul, were selected to prepare the final re-use scheme. This creates facilities for a new 250-seat auditorium, for shops, restaurants, art galleries, and it provides offices for the Arts and Science Council and its members. It also provides for restoration of not just the original three but four courtrooms, and, perhaps most important of all for the public's perception of the building, the high central court of the building has now been restored. This space, which is shown on the previous page, originally had three ceilings—one at the very top, another two floors below that, and one between the first and second floors to provide security for the post office that used to be there. The lower ceiling has now been removed, giving for the first time the chance for the visitor on the first floor to see this remarkable space in a single glance. In the space directly below the roof at the very top a greenhouse enlivens what was formerly an attic, as the plans on this and the following page illustrate. It is surrounded by a museum art school and by additional space still unassigned, waiting for some future occupants.

Though still not yet fully complete, the Old Federal Courts Building has been sufficiently refurbished, sufficiently altered, and sufficiently loved so that it has now become the Landmark Center its supporters and creators wanted it to be. It is worth noting that there are now other similar projects under way because of the 1972 amendment to the Surplus Property Act. But it is also worth noting that there are still other projects—like the renovation of the Old Federal Building in St. Louis or of the Customhouse in New York—which are *not* under way (or if they are, under different sails) because no suitable local takers could be found. Nothing worthwhile happens quite automatically, and so while it seems certainly fair to say that GSA's initiative in the Surplus Property Act was imaginative, so does it have to be said that the citizens of St. Paul deserve due credit for their persistence in realizing its possibilities—as well as, perhaps, in helping to create the environment for it in the first place.

Shin Koyama photos

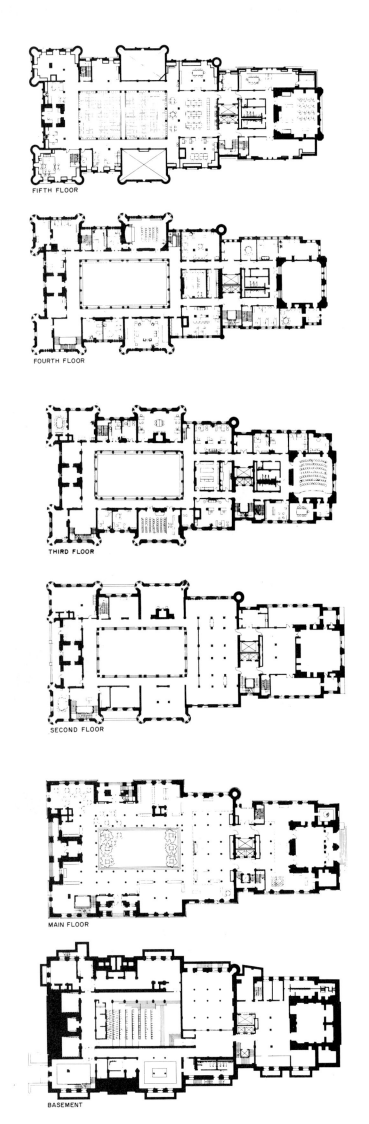

FIFTH FLOOR

FOURTH FLOOR

THIRD FLOOR

SECOND FLOOR

MAIN FLOOR

BASEMENT

The color photograph on the opposite page shows the restored law library in Landmark Center. The lighting was re-created from early photographs, and other details were handled with equal meticulousness in this purely restorational part of the project. Also restored was the Superior Court room shown on the left. The photograph on the right shows the marble foyer under the north tower, and the photographs above show the arcades around the central court inside.

Shin Koyama photos

THE ST. LOUIS ART MUSEUM

Cass Gilbert was the original architect of the St. Louis Art Museum completed in 1904. Like other American Beaux Arts architects he looked to ancient Rome in his search for the timeless architectural values which he hoped to bring to his work. For his vast St. Louis project, designed as part of the St. Louis Exposition, he decided that the Thermae of Caracalla had a spatial order which would be just right. (A few years later McKim, Mead and White were to turn to the same source for Pennsylvania Station). He fashioned the combined concourse and sculpture hall of the museum (right and page 13) after the tepidarium. As in the Roman bath, the hall has three great bays with arched recesses at opposite ends of each bay. The whole is roofed by a barrel vault interrupted by lunettes. At each end of the main axis are three arched doorways spanned by a balcony and crowned by a lunette. All of these elements, thanks to the perceptions and craft of Hugh Hardy, Malcolm Holzman and Norman Pfeiffer have become readable once more and a magnificent room has emerged. The architects, who call what they do ''interpretive restoration,'' have also re-discovered and successfully restated the formal dynamics of other spaces within the museum. They clearly love the building. In Hugh Hardy's words: ''This major work by a once-forgotten architect gives delight in its audacity and solidity, its remembrance of the past and its commitment to the future.''

There are not many architects still alive who received Beaux Arts training before 1930—the date which marks the ending of the influence of the Ecole des Beaux Arts in the United States. In the last four decades, those among them who believed that the birth of the Modern Movement heralded the death of true Architecture were little heeded when they spoke with admiration of the work of Henry Hornbostel, Stanford White, Paul Cret, John Russell Pope, Ralph Adams Cram, Bertram Goodhue, Cass Gilbert and the rest.

The few older architects who are still around to enjoy watching the younger practitioners discover Goodhue and Gilbert must also envy them their opportunities to restore fine eclectic buildings—chances these same young architects are eagerly seizing.

During the thirties, forties, fifties and sixties in the United States most alterations or additions to beautiful old buildings were depredations performed by architects for whom the eclectic work had little meaning or value. Today, more of the public, more owners, and more architects value our heritage of buildings which predate the Modern Movement and contemporary architectural styles. And more architects—through their historical and theoretical studies which are today's substitutes for Beaux Arts training—have begun to understand the formal dynamics of the historical styles.

This is a hopeful sign. Much critical attention is now being paid to the influences of a given architect's historical and theoretical understanding upon his original creative work. Just as important, however, is the influence of this understanding upon the buildings and urban environments which he is now being invited to repair or transform.

Today, because of energy concerns, the cost of new buildings, and the heightened awareness of the value of our architectural heritage, many architects get more invitations to fix an old building than to build a new one. A grand old state capitol, court house, post office, library or museum that needs a new roof usually also needs air conditioning, new plumbing and wiring and improved lighting.

Often this is all the client wants, but if the building is of architectural quality, the good architect tries to do more. He raises the level of dialogue with his client by helping him discover the building's timeless formal values, persuading him to restore these too. Another dialogue must then begin between the architect who will restore and the predecessor who designed a building with the strength to survive its own time.

Hugh Hardy, the partner-in-charge of the $6.6 million St. Louis restoration, immersed himself in the life and work of Cass Gilbert. Though he was one of America's most famous Beaux Arts architects, Gilbert never studied at the Ecole des Beaux Arts. He died in 1934 at the age of seventy-four. He was then what we call today an establishment figure, helping found the Architectural League in 1881, serving as its president, and becoming the president of the AIA. For good measure he served as president of the National Academy of Design and as a trustee of the Metropolitan Museum of Art.

His fame barely outlasted his life, for as a leading eclectic he was to be ignored by the polemicists of the Modern Movement who began to be heard in the decade of his death, and this eclipse of his reputation demonstrates the exclusionary power of polemic. Gilbert had, after all, designed the Woolworth Building (once the world's tallest) and the United States Custom House in New York, the United States Supreme Court Building in Washington, D.C., the St. Louis Public Library, in 1933 an arts building for Oberlin College (made famous once more because of a highly controversial addition by Robert Venturi), and many other commercial, institutional and governmental buildings.

Hugh Hardy believes that many of these projects established an eminent style which was widely copied. A re-assessment of Gilbert's work would help illuminate a period that the historians have neglected for too long. HHP's brilliant restoration of the St. Louis Art Museum should instigate the process.

The museum began as an integral part of a much grander scheme which Gilbert composed for the 1904 Exposition. It became a freestanding permanent masonry building displaying U.S. painting and plaster casts of sculpture as part of the Fair's complex devoted to the fine arts. During the Fair it was surrounded by temporary stucco pavilions displaying the art of Great Britain, Germany, Holland, Belgium, Italy and France. These temporary pavilions were later removed.

Although, as already noted, the art museum derives the form of its main hall from the Thermae of Caracalla, its galleries are not spanned by Roman masonry vaults. Gilbert made the most of the techniques available to him at the time and roofed his vast skylit galleries with steel trusses, using industrial building techniques.

Many neo-classic museums built around the turn of the century are composed in a manner similar to St. Louis with lower exhibition halls symmetrically arranged on opposite sides of a high vaulted central hall. Hardy points out, however, that "although Gilbert's spatial arrangement cannot be called unique, it is remarkably subtle in the way a variety of skylit volumes manipulates natural light. It is these contrasts between a central 38-foot-tall

gallery and others of 24 feet and 18 feet—some on the north, some on the south, some with clerestories, some with windows; each offering a different intensity and color of light—that distinguish his design. And it is from both the reinforcement of the axial plan and the celebration of natural light that our present restoration takes its premise.''

Hardy Holzman Pfeiffer's success in St. Louis was rooted as much in the firm's technological sophistication as in its grasp of the subtleties of Gilbert's design. Their first task was to respond to the museum's need for a better physical environment for its art.

By 1973, soon after the restoration and new construction program began, the building's original skylights, then 69 years old, were badly corroded. Rain leaked through them and they admitted far too much daylight for proper conservation of the art. The artificial lighting was entirely inadequate, wall and ceiling surfaces were in bad repair, and the floor surfaces were an ill-assorted collection of materials—marble, soapstone, tile, and wood, which failed to reinforce the geometric order of the Beaux Arts plan. Here and there were doorways and furnishings of today's dimensions, looking dinky and forlorn in the vast rooms. So many ill-proportioned spaces had been installed within Gilbert's halls and rooms that it required today's equivalent of Beaux Arts training to sense the presence of a once vigorously legible order.

As we now see, it was all there: rectangles within rectangles forming the well-articulated network of halls, vestibules and stairs connecting rooms related to each other within a carefully graded hierarchy of volumes. HHP's restoration allows the public once again to be accommodated grandly, invited to make its way on foot up the main staircase and into the Sculpture Hall and on into spaces designed to be experienced as walked through—fine passages forming a succession of axes, cross axes and cross-cross axes.

Although the architects were invited to restore only the galleries to the southeast of the Sculpture Hall, there they have made a consequential gesture toward re-establishing the building's symmetry.

The axes once more accommodate sight as well as movement. On the principal facade a niche was transformed into a window to provide a view down a secondary axis of the building to the surrounding park (photos right). By this adjustment HHP improved Gilbert's building by honoring in one more way the Beaux Arts principle that the composition of the interior be made manifest on the exterior.

For this project, appropriately, the architects did everything possible to conceal the sophisticated new climate control and security systems required to meet the standards of environmental quality for today's museums. All such equipment has been located within the original walls and fan rooms and in a new partially buried concrete structure.

Connoisseurs of HHP's exposed ductwork painted lavender or green must look hard to find a single specimen in the St. Louis restoration. There is an exposed duct in the print gallery—a personal signature. It is lavender and the only one.

THE ST. LOUIS ART MUSEUM, St. Louis, Missouri. Architects: *Hardy Holzman Pfeiffer Associates—partner-in-charge: Hugh Hardy;* project architect: *Alec W. Gibson.* Consultants: *Peckham & Guyton* (field architects); *LeMessurier Associates/SCI* (structural); *Crawford & White* (mechanical); *Van & Vierse* (electrical); *Jules Fisher & Paul Marantz, Inc.* (lighting). Construction manager: *Howard Needles Tammen & Bergendoff, Inc.* General contractor: *Dickie Construction Co.*

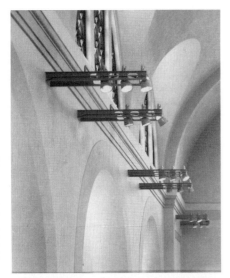

A key problem for the architects and their lighting consultants, Jules Fisher & Paul Marantz, Inc., was how to mediate between their desire to retain Cass Gilbert's beautiful daylit spaces and their knowledge of the destructive qualities of such light to works of art. Helping Hardy Holzman Pfeiffer establish new lighting standards for the St. Louis Art Museum and meeting them became a technical and esthetic challenge. In the words of Paul Marantz:

A museum is a building about seeing. Nowhere is light more critical to the success of an interior space and its program than here. The St. Louis Art Museum preceded the electric era in concept and chronology. The existing interior architecture offered little guidance for the introduction of electric lighting, which in earlier attempts had been glued on or dangled in. Neither was there any historical vocabulary of light fittings in reasonable scale to the enormous spaces, which would have provided the plastic flow of light we have learned to use.

On the other hand, Cass Gilbert was deeply concerned with daylight and brought it into his museum in ingenious ways. He incorporated an extensive system of skylights/laylights in every gallery, and clerestory windows in the great Sculpture Hall. Our problem as lighting designers was to retain the daylit spaces while removing the art destroying qualities of the daylight itself.

We made a big reduction in the quantity of daylight and completely eliminated ultraviolet radiation since it does not contribute to seeing. Now the interior wall illumination by daylight is equal to about one half of one per cent of the exterior daylight available on the roof. We achieved this by installing glass and louver sandwiches in both the skylight and laylight. These reduce, filter, and redistribute the daylight so that the largest quantity of light is focused in the hanging zone on the lower portions of the walls, thus enhancing the pictures.*

The viewer's eye will tell him that this vastly reduced illumination is equal to daylight as long as no clues remain to give away the deception. Therefore, we fitted every window and door with the appropriate light-absorbent glass to maintain direct exterior views in the proper scalar relationship to the gallery top lighting. The Sculpture Hall is used as a light conditioning room, in which the eye adjusts from outdoor brightness to the low light levels of the galleries.

A system to provide for gallery lighting by daylight alone would properly require mechanical regulation of the light intensity to prevent either destructively high levels in summer, or gloom in winter and on overcast days. Budget, our lack of faith in inaccessible

machinery, and belief that the caprices of daylight are a virtue, suggested to us that the daylight system be designed passively for the 90th percentile clear summer day and that an incandescent electric light system be used to support the daylight as required. Thus daylight and electric light (which is not "artificial," conventional language notwithstanding) were considered as one complementary system.

The units of hardware designed for the incandescent system are among the few contemporary images (apart from certain art works) included in the building. We emphasized this modern intrusion upon the turn-of-the century structure by clearly separating the two, detaching the tracks and other lighting elements from the building envelope. In Sculpture Hall, cantilevered brackets hold the lighting units away from the masonry walls. We carefully considered how big we should design the entire assembly of each unit to be in scale with the immense room. We also made a great many studies to find the proper scale for the lighting fixtures in the galleries.

The only concealed lighting we installed consists of some uplighting for the lower side vaults, end vaults, and lunettes of Sculpture Hall to give the space plasticity and greater interest at night.

The illumination of the St. Louis Art Museum differs significantly from that of other recently built museums. Louis Kahn's two last museums, for example, are lit differently from St. Louis and from each other, with our solution for St. Louis directly in between. The Kimball Museum in Fort Worth admits far less daylight than the British Art Center at Yale University which has largely daylit galleries. While the St. Louis Art Museum admits less than one-third of the daylight allowed into the Yale building, it—like the Kahn museum—gives the impression of abundant daylight filling the space.

---

*In the new skylight installation, insulating glass was used to reduce heat loss. The outer layer is a tempered gray glass to reduce the total transmittance of daylight. The lower layer is a white opal glass to diffuse the light and serve as a cover for the light dispersion box or attic which has been painted white.

The laylights at the ceiling level have a top layer which consists of an opal ultraviolet shield of acrylic plastic. In addition to screening out the harmful ultraviolet rays this layer keeps dust out of the louver directly below it and will act as a safety net in the unlikely event of skylight breakage. The louver is approximately .650 inches deep with 3/8 inch hexagonal cells which direct light downward and even the light distribution. A two-inch air space between the louver and the lower layer of stippled tempered glass helps conceal the louver pattern from below. The new ceiling assembly was prefabricated in aluminum frames and dropped into the existing ceiling framework.

Through the 74-year life of the museum, Cass Gilbert's design was little understood, and many depredations were made upon it (top and left). HHP began by removing these piecemeal accretions, thus re-stating Gilbert's axial and spatial themes. The main axis (overleaf) and the minor axis (opposite page) were clarified and enhanced. The museum insisted that the fountain at the crossing of the two axes remain and the architects agreed. Though not part of Cass Gilbert's original design, it helps turn the concourse from a channel to a room. By making the most of the fountain, HHP had all of architectural and town planning wisdom behind them, for every intersection of paths of movement is transformed by a monument or fountain as a place to stop and be.

The architects investigated Gilbert's ornament and color palettes in buildings in which they were better preserved than in the art museum (the St. Louis Public library for an example). They found that he loved bright colors and rich decorative devices. The Sculpture Hall once had a highly patterned tile ceiling. Despite what they learned, HHP elected to use color and ornament sparingly in the belief that color and decoration of extreme subtlety was better suited to today's esthetic standards. The over-all effect has the delicacy in color and light of a fine drawing in the Beaux Arts manner.

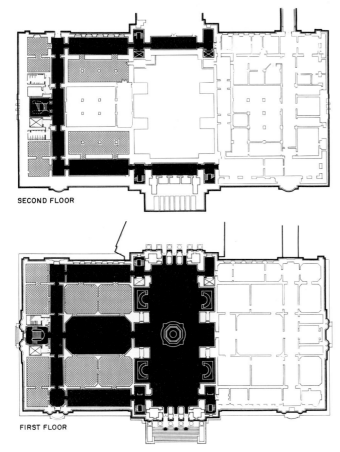

SECOND FLOOR

FIRST FLOOR

Cass Gilbert's axes form a lattice of movement which surrounds and contains the exhibition spaces. Down through the years, no one seems to have understood the architectural significance of this lattice or how it worked. Museum curators who should have known better cluttered these passages, blocked them off, sealed their windows and created fake period environments for their genuine art— making it difficult to distinguish between the two (top and left).

In order to re-establish the lattice, HHP had to cut new openings in certain walls and restore existing doorways and frames. All the openings and walls in the transformed main floor areas have new moldings copied from Gilbert's own profiles. The architects elected to restore this much of the ornament to introduce elements of appropriate scale within the huge volumes of the rooms. Doorways less grand than these would have looked hopelessly forlorn.

Where necessary the elegant doorways contain smoke alarm-activated, roll-down fire doors. These doors are carefully integrated into the delicately molded frames. Their presence is revealed by a nearly concealed one inch slot in the head and jambs.

The vista at right is a view from the Sculpture Hall, through a principal gallery to the hall containing the main staircase beyond. The gallery for smaller sculpture (below left) is parallel to the main facade.

The gallery (below right) has casework and moldings by Gilbert and murals by Elmer Garnsey. This square, domed room is lit by an oculus (not shown).

Cass Gilbert's skylights (section below) were re-constructed, re-glazed and augmented by incandescent light. The quantity of daylight was greatly reduced and the combined light better directed to the lower or viewing portions of the walls. A detailed account of the lighting solution is given on page 11. The museum was not originally designed for electric light, but an early incandescent system (above) was temporarily put in place for the 1904 St. Louis Exposition.

The museum required a new grand staircase (right) which HHP executed in an altogether contemporary manner. Nonetheless, by its sinuous curve, and dark rich colors it makes a gesture toward Gilbert's classicism.

A gallery on the second floor, one of two skylit studios which Gilbert had designed as places to give art classes, was used for storage (left) until this restoration. It is now the major new gallery for the display of prints, drawings and photographs (below). Its skylight has been reglazed with two layers of solar glass and fitted with louver blinds.

All wall surfaces throughout the renovation upon which paintings are hung have been resurfaced with 32-ply birch plywood, a surface easily repaired after the removal of paintings.

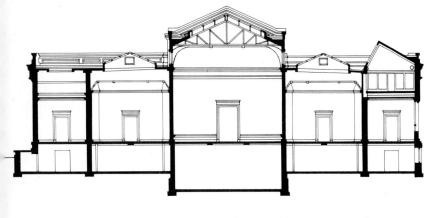

Cass Gilbert's southwest facade was partially concealed by an auditorium and service facilities added in the fifties which ignored the museum's major axis and violated its symmetry (top and left). Hardy Holzman Pfeiffer were asked to devise a master plan for the development of further facilities for administrative, curatorial and library functions on the southwest. They took this as an opportunity to improve the connections and scale relationships between the original building and the additions.

HHP's proposal (which was carried out by Kivett and Myers) called for the three unit, stepped level structure shown in the site plan and model photos. The auditorium is concealed within the skin of the middle unit. The architects believe that the new spaces need not have the monumental character of Cass Gilbert's work. Their proposal was carried out as a brick masonry envelope which encloses an open simple interior with windows overlooking the park.

Now that work is completed, the Cass Gilbert building is once more freestanding. Instead of the awkward connection which disfigured the facade, a new sculpture terrace joins the new and existing construction. Serving also as an extension of a restaurant, this terrace provides a direct connection among all the areas of the museum at the lower level of the Gilbert building.

The main axis has been re-established by the restoration of the original south stairs and the provision of an avenue of trees accessible from the parking area.

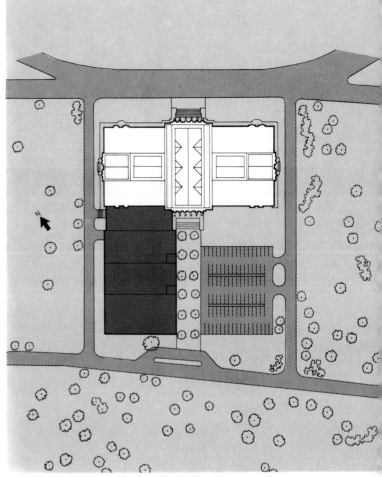

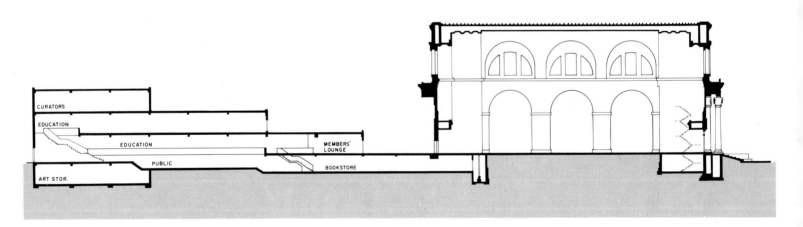

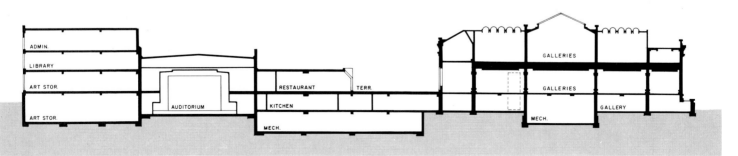

ARTS AND INDUSTRIES BUILDING

The Arts and Industries Building of the Smithsonian Institution was begun in 1879 and opened soon after. With guidance from the Smithsonian's architectural and engineering staff and consulting architect Hugh Newell Jacobsen, the great but tragically neglected old building was renewed for the Bicentennial. The museum's curators installed an entirely new exhibition of Victorian artifacts, some of which were originally shown to commemorate the nation's 100th birthday at the famous 1876 Exposition in Philadelphia. The 1976 exhibition was designed less to teach about the past than to give the experience of having been in it. Its great popular success owed much to the behind-the-scenes work of Jacobsen, who elected not to attempt a literal restoration of the interiors, but to recapture the essence of their late 19th-century expression.

The "exposition" as an idea is a 19th-century phenomenon originating in the desire on the part of government and industry to inform and excite the public about technological and industrial advances. So important culturally were these exhibits devoted to the products of industry, that the most important of them gave a name to and thus helped define the style of the time. Until the end of the 19th century, styles were named after kings, emperors and an occasional queen. Now, most classifiers in the fields of 19th and 20th century architecture and the fine and decorative arts will, wherever possible, label the design of a period with the name of its most important exhibition. Thus we have the style of the Paris Exposition Universelle of 1900, which has its roots in some of the artifacts shown in London's Great Exhibition of 1851 held in Joseph Paxton's Crystal Palace. In the United States, the revival of neoclassicism was heralded by the Chicago World's Fair of 1893.

Less famous but of great cultural importance, nonetheless, was the 1876 Exposition in Philadelphia's Fairmont Park. No previous fair had so effectively presented the growing inventive genius of the United States. The Arts and Industries Building in Washington, D.C. was originally constructed by the Smithsonian to house boxcar loads of objects from this exposition, which had been transported from Philadelphia by steam engine and dumped on the Mall. (Most of these artifacts were eventually discarded.) In 1976, in honor of the Bicentennial, the Smithsonian used the Arts and Industries Building as the setting for an exhibition that evoked the spirit of the 1876 Centennial. The show included approximately 25,000 objects of this period, 15 per cent of which were actually from the Centennial Exposition.

A careful restoration of the Arts and Industries Building was long overdue and the installation of the Bicentennial exhibit made it essential. Before Victorian structures began to re-emerge as objects of beauty and curiosity, the Arts and Industries Building had been treated with contempt, in part because of the ascendance of the neo-classic style launched at the 1893 Chicago World's Fair just noted. Even when it opened, in 1881, it had not been thought very much of in spite of the fact that it was the first government building to be electrified. It had the misfortune of having been built cheaply (for $3.20 per square foot) and was indeed Washington's most inexpensively constructed public building. Designed by Adolph Cluss and Rudolph Schulze, who had been doing schools, it was their first major structure, and they rigorously kept costs down. Cruciform in plan with four similar facades, it has no basement and an open steel joist ceiling. Except for the central rotunda and the four entrance halls, which were laid in encaustic tile, most of the floors were originally of wood.

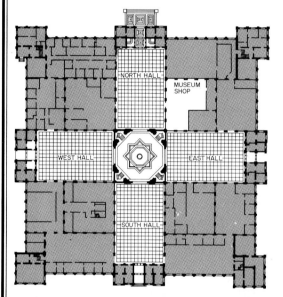

The drawing above shows the west hall as it appeared in 1881, the year the Arts and Industries Building opened. The occasion was the Inaugural Ball for President James Garfield. The balconies that appear in the recent photo (opposite page) were added around 1910. The design of the new stencils over the arches is similar to those in the drawing and were based upon careful study of old photographs with a jeweler's loupe. The plan (left) is current, and shows a Victorian fountain, added by Jacobsen, where a fountain always should have been, but never was before. All of the artifacts (below and page 2) have been painted and shined to look like new.

22

The budget permitted the restoration of only one of the Arts and Industries Building's four facades, and the front entry (above) was the logical choice. The work included cleaning and renewing the ornamentation, replacing damaged brick in the vestibule and installing a new set of oak and walnut doors (right). The old photograph (left) served as one of the references for the exterior restoration.

Early records indicate that the building was exceedingly uncomfortable. In the first nine years, ten Smithsonian employees died of influenza and the damp wood floors laid on grade were blamed. These floors were gradually replaced with marble tiles.

In the 95 years that elapsed between the first opening day and the spring of 1976, the fine old building had been altered many times, but never until 1976 in a way which even observed, much less enhanced, its true esthetic qualities. Because of his successful restoration for the Smithsonian of the Renwick, architect Hugh Jacobsen was commissioned by Paul N. Perrot, Assistant Secretary for Museum Programs, to deal with the now recognized esthetic and stylistic aspects of the most recent remodeling. Meanwhile the in-house Office of Facilities Planning and Engineering Services was hard at work solving the general problems connected with heating, ventilating, air conditioning and upgrading the physical fabric of the structure.

Jacobsen began by considering and then dismissing the question as to which of its many past guises the interior should be restored, because the interiors had never been decorated in a unified style. "They had hacks back then too," says he, "and they made mistakes." No single interior renovation, as examined in old (1880-1890) photographs with the aid of a jeweler's loupe seemed just right to Jacobsen, but some of the details did, including the encaustic tile floor, already mentioned, which had been removed and discarded except for the west entry hall. The problem as Jacobsen saw it was to select, assemble and reproduce only those details which best evoked the spirit of the Victorian structure. A literal restoration of the interiors as they appeared at any one time would not only have been prohibitive in cost, but also an esthetic disaster.

A comparison of the photographs of the renovation with early photographs (far left and below right) indicates that Jacobsen's approach was successful. Although he did not design the exhibition itself (this was done by the Arts and Industries Building's curatorial staff), Jacobsen and his project architect, Paul B. Pavlovich, were responsible for the stenciling, flooring, hardware, colors, fenestration, doors, graphics and lighting (other than the hanging chandeliers). The interior colors match samples discovered under seven or eight layers of paint. The colors of the stenciling were selected in the same manner with the aid of extensive reading of contemporary correspondence in the Smithsonian Institution archives.

ARTS AND INDUSTRIES BUILDING, Washington, D.C. Owner: *The Smithsonian Institution.* Architect: *Hugh Newell Jacobsen—Paul B. Pavlovich* (project architect); associated architects: *The Smithsonian Institution, Office of Facilities Planning and Engineering Services, Engineering and Design Branch—William L. Thomas* (architect-in-charge). General contractor: *Grunley-Walsh Construction Co., Inc.* Principal subcontractors: *H. & R. Johnson, Inc.* (ceramic tile fabricator); *Standard Art Marble and Tile Co.* (tile installer); *Myers-Christiansen Co.* (wall stencilwork).

The old photograph (left) was made on a glass negative, now cracked. It shows the original encaustic tile floor in the central rotunda, and the decorated frieze below the dome. The photos (above and overleaf) show the new Jacobsen designed stencils, the newly installed Victorian fountain, and the new encaustic tile floor. The process of duplicating the old tile floor was a formidable one. Determining the exact sizes, shapes and colors was difficult as Jacobsen and his team had only a half dozen or so original photos to work from. Finding the source for the encaustic tile was particularly difficult since the method of producing it had been universally abandoned in the mid-thirties. Enquiries were sent to almost all tile firms in the United States, Europe and Mexico. Only two firms were willing to experiment with encaustic tile production, and after one year of these experiments, the job was given to H & R Johnson, Inc., in Great Britain, who are the successors to the firm which laid the original tiles in the Arts and Industries Building. In brief, the re-discovered process consists of stamping a so-called "green" tile with a patterned die, firing it, filling the depressed area with one or more pigmented clays and refiring it.

KATONAH STATION RESTAURANT

While the 19th-century railroad Station at Katonah, New York, scarcely qualifies as landmark architecture, it has, like its more splendid sisters around the country, received the benefit of tender restoration and adaptive use.

At the new Katonah Station Restaurant, the main dining room occupies the old baggage room, where, when travel was more leisurely, luggage was held until it was claimed. Architect Myron Goldfinger retained the utilitarian tongue-and-groove board walls, after sandblasting them to remove half a century's accumulation of paint. He also enlarged the opening into the bar (formerly the waiting room), designing an arched opening to echo existing vaulting and lunette in the area now given to the private dining room (at right in plan).

Because the trains still stop at Katonah—it is a functioning commuter station—it was a condition of the project that the building be open to passengers between 6 and 10 o'clock in the morning. During those hours, tables and chairs are removed from the private dining room and an adjacent alcove; and the banquettes, which Goldfinger fashioned from the old waiting room benches, resume their original purpose. After the commuter rush, the restaurant staff returns the banquette pillows and sets up for lunch.

Restaurant clientele enters through a new door at the front of the building, and is guided by the diagonal bar to the main dining room. Passengers enter the waiting room at the back of the building through a door to the train platform.

KATONAH STATION RESTAURANT, Katonah, New York. Owner: *Ira Marcus*. Architect: *Myron Goldfinger*.

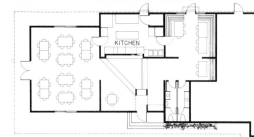

Norman McGrath photos

27

CUSTOM HOUSE BLOCK AND CHART HOUSE RESTAURANT

The two buildings shown in the photo (upper left) are situated on Boston's Long Wharf and linger as a link with the city's 18th century past. The larger of the two, the old Custom House, has already been placed on the National Register of historic places, but by 1966 was largely vacant and neglected. Boston architects Anderson Notter Associates were commissioned to convert the four-story granite building into 27 luxury apartment units. Transverse masonry walls actually separated the structure into nine separate buildings—each with a full attic. The architects pierced these walls with new arches to let corridors through. Modern egress stairs and a new elevator shaft were installed. New electrical services, central heating, sprinklers and intercom system were also installed. The massive timbers framing the roof were exposed in the attic duplexes and old masonry walls were cleaned with care. Because of the building's configuration, each apartment is spatially unique and looks out over the old Boston waterfront in a broad vista of water and shipping.

The smaller building, adjacent to the Custom House, was purchased by a West Coast restaurant chain that specializes in broiled seafood and steak. Because of the restrictions placed on the project by the Historic District, the exteriors were retained very nearly intact. Using the same technique they employed in the Custom House, Anderson Notter cut through transverse walls of the three existing bays and built new arches from old brick removed to make the openings. Brick walls were sandblasted and old timber joists were exposed and cleaned. The lowest level is used as a cocktail lounge; the second floor and mezzanine serve as dining spaces. A manager's office and support spaces occupy the old attic and create the uppermost partial level seen in the section (top right).

Both conversions were executed with very considerable design concern and with respect for the virtues of the original structures. The result is that two historic buildings, suffering from long neglect, are now restored to usefulness and a disintegrating portion of the city is starting to feel the quickening pulse of new waterfront activity.

CUSTOM HOUSE BLOCK AND CHART HOUSE RESTAURANT, Boston, Massachusetts. Architects: *Anderson Notter Associates, Inc.* Engineers: *Arthur Choo Associates* (structural); *W. N. Peterson Associates, Inc.* (mechanical); *Joseph V. Herosy* (electrical). Contractor: *Stoneholm Construction Company.*

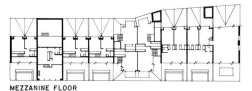

MEZZANINE FLOOR

FIFTH FLOOR

15

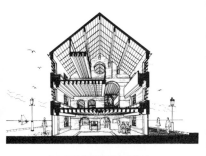

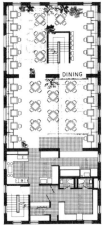

SECOND FLOOR

GROUND FLOOR   5

The three structural bays that
formed the original building are still
visible in the plans although
the architects pierced the transverse
walls with new arched openings.
Restaurant use, to conform with local
codes, was restricted to the
middle two floors, and the street floor
is used as a cocktail lounge.

The detailing of new work
throughout is consistent but not fussy
so that it matches, in spirit at least,
the shims and ad hoc character of
the original framing,
much of which was concealed before
renovation. Nothing seems quite plumb
in the old building and the
architects made a virtue
of these eccentricities in the
renovation.

Stephen Dunham and Kiku Obata photos

OFFICE FOR HELLMUTH, OBATA & KASSABAUM

HOK'S San Francisco office is in a part of the city between downtown and Telegraph Hill where renovation and adaptive use are the rage— an area characterized by large brick warehouse buildings ready to be turned to more glamorous commercial use. In this case the intention was to create a simple kind of space where there could be a heterogeneous mix of employees without the usual distinctions between front and back room. So the major part of the space is given over to one open office area (photo above) where members of the staff have their own work stations defined by low partitions. This large space is on the building perimeter, with exposure to natural light. On the inside wall there are three offices that offer more privacy (photo below) and a conference room.

OFFICE FOR HELLMUTH, OBATA & KASSABAUM, San Francisco, California. Architects: *Hellmuth, Obata & Kassabaum—project team: Gyo Obata, Dan Gale, Bill Valentine and Bob Stauder.* Contractor: *Balliet Brothers Construction Corporation.*

OLD PAVILION, STANFORD UNIVERSITY

Jeremiah O. Bragstad photos

At Stanford University, an old unused campus gymnasium was recycled to provide badly-needed office space for two university departments. The restored building's rich new interior is an elegant mixture of brick, wood and steel, glowing with color.

The 2,700-seat Stanford Old Pavilion, built in 1921, had fallen into disuse a decade ago after a larger multi-purpose sports center was completed. With its interior sprayed entirely a dingy off-white, the Pavilion had temporarily provided a drab setting for some campus offices before university officials decided to have the building converted to permanent office space.

The 17,000 square foot gymnasium with its 48-foot ceiling presented interior designer Barry Brukoff with problems ranging from severe acoustical reverberations to erratic heating. Brukoff, who thought the building's interior volume "reminiscent of some of the turn-of-the-century train stations—raw, but in its own way quite elegant," wanted to restore as much of the original interior as possible while providing a handsome work space for the personnel and architectural planning departments.

Sandblasting the entire structure, Brukoff began by exposing the original red brick, steel beams, and natural redwood. The clerestory windows were also sandblasted to produce a frosted glass that would cut direct sunlight on work areas. The exposed roof area was insulated and finished with rough-sawn fir plywood.

The University had asked that the Pavilion's fine old basketball floor be preserved in case it was needed in the future, but the floor was too springy to simply carpet for office use. To provide a more solid floor and allow room for underfloor wiring, new 2 by 6 framing with plywood flooring was constructed on top of the basketball floor, and the two floors were fastened together, stiffening the whole area.

Brukoff added an elevated platform at the entryway to provide a reception area, lounge, and space for a large-scale model of the campus used by the planning department. A balcony along the north wall was also constructed to set private conference space apart from the regular open-plan office on the floor.

Brukoff began the luxurious coloring of the interior by painting the ceiling's steel beams a glossy white to heighten their lacy quality against the wood roof, and countered with soft cadet blue along the balcony and

Freestanding walls and integrated office systems were used to divide the Pavilion's immense space for use by two different offices. A balcony (below) was constructed along one wall to provide private conference space, and noisy office machines were grouped under canopies to confine noise. The raised entry platform (left bottom) provides a reception area, lounge, and space for a model used by the planning department.

34

walls. Warming the room with russet carpeting, he stretched a 150-foot ivy bed along the balcony and entryway, and painted the air-handling ducts overhead a deep red. The soldier-course masonry arch over the window was accented with a band of dark purple.

The enormous space required special lighting, so custom tubular 18 inch diameter fixtures were designed and installed running along both sides of the building, and metal-halide fixtures were suspended from the high center bay, with task lighting added at work stations.

To allow two different departments to share the new interior, the building was divided by freestanding wood walls, which can be moved in the future as office needs change. The open-plan offices on both sides of the wall reflect the difference in the two departments' work; personnel offices are arranged in an angular, free-form manner while the planning offices are in a linear grid dictated by the need for large drafting tables and plan files.

Integrated office systems throughout lend a sense of unity, and panels separating offices are below standing eye-level to promote spaciousness, but above seated eye-level for privacy.

To solve the acoustic problems, Brukoff controlled office machinery and files—two primary noisemakers —by grouping them together and surrounding them with freestanding walls. Pale brick-colored canopies were then hung over the enclosed area to absorb and confine sound.

The final effect, that of luxuriant spaciousness, has become a source of pride for university employees working in the building. "I enjoy walking into it in the morning and to some extend I regret leaving in the evening," said the co-director of the planning department. "Many times I'm the one to turn off all the lights. And invariably, when there's nothing on except the night lights, I come back in and just stand on the platform and enjoy it, because it's quite dramatic with just a spot of light here and a spot of light there."

OLD PAVILION, STANFORD UNIVERSITY, Stanford, California. Owner: *Trustees of Stanford University.* Designer: *Barry Brukoff.* Consulting architect: *Michael Wolfe Siegel.* Consultants: *Pregnoff, Matheu & Lee (structural); Westcon Associates (mechanical); David Arrigoni & Associates (electrical).* Contractor: *Howard J. White Inc.*

WINCHESTER CATHEDRAL TREASURY/ NORWICH CATHEDRAL TREASURY

The cathedrals of England and the parish churches of their dioceses often possess beautiful and valuable collections of old silver and gold—chalices, patens, basins, ewers and other objects used in ecclesiastical ceremony. Until recently in modern times, these were almost always kept stashed away in bank vaults, available on loan for special exhibitions or brought out occasionally for major church festivals. Well over a decade ago, however, the idea of cathedral treasuries—special places where these collections could be displayed—was advocated and underwritten by the Worshipful Company of Goldsmiths, a semiofficial, benevolent band of craftsmen and enthusiasts roughly equivalent in essence if not in style to an American professional association. The first cathedral treasury, at Lincoln, was opened in 1960, and since then treasuries have been installed at Winchester, Norwich and York. Those at Winchester and Norwich were designed by London architects Stefan Buzas and Alan Irvine, and they are shown on this and the following page.

Edgar Hyman and Peter Charley photos

The single bronze display case of the Winchester Cathedral treasury, seen close up and from above and below in the adjacent photographs, has eight separate sections; the bottom is lined with Purbeck stone, whose light color reflects the light from the chandelier suspended above.

The Winchester treasury, shown on this page, is in a small 15th-century gallery above the nave of the cathedral near the west door; the entrance is by a small door and a short winding stairway. In the gallery is a single showcase elegantly constructed of bronze; its translucent glass top admits light from the 16-lamp chandelier suspended above. The chandelier is made of bronze-anodized aluminum to minimize its weight. The central, cruciform-plan showcase was chosen in order to give adequate circulation space around the case and to leave the balustrades clear and thus to preserve two excellent views of the cathedral.

The Norwich treasury, shown on this page, is also situated in an existing gallery—this one in the ambulatory of the cathedral, and possessed of notable 14th-century frescoes on the vaults above. There are four display cases, of which two form part of the glass walls within the semicircular arches enclosing the treasury. Above each of these showcases is a seven-light bracket made of bronze. There is also a shallow showcase in the north wall, and a central showcase, whose lighting also illuminates the frescoes on the ceiling.

WINCHESTER CATHEDRAL TREASURY, Winchester, England; NORWICH CATHEDRAL TREASURY, Norwich, England. Architects: *Stefan Buzas and Alan Irvine.* Engineers: *Ove Arups* (structural, for reinforced concrete vault at Winchester). Prime contractor: *A. Edmonds & Co.* (for fabrication of bronze showcases).

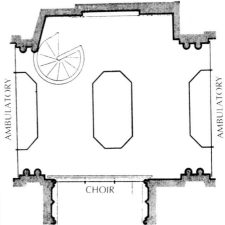

The Norwich Cathedral treasury was installed in a gallery above the north choir aisle, used in medieval times for the display of relics, and enclosed now by glass walls, making the treasury visible from below. The architects of the treasury also designed the iron gate at its entrance.

OPP
RESIDENCE

An aging but still substantial brick rowhouse at the end of a residential block in St. Paul was the starting point for this elaborate residential renovation by the Design Consortium. Of the original interior, only the ornamental mantle, the stair to the upper level and the bathroom plumbing connections were retained. All else is new. The architects began by creating an upper and lower apartment, the lower making splendid use of what had been the 11-foot-high basement space (photo opposite). To make this basement volume fully habitable, the architects threw it open to the level above and borrowed light from the first floor windows. The result is a beautiful space keyed to all the other smaller spaces by carefully studied transitional elements. The delicacy of touch in this renovation is remarkable as is the intelligent use of color to reinforce the linear character of the design and the skillful development of secondary circulation on the raised gallery above.

The upper (entry) level provides a private bedroom at the rear, a more open bedroom overlooking the living room, and a private study reached by a warp in the line of the gallery (see photos).

The upper level apartment, when complete, will be a rental unit.

The Opp residence is another superb reminder that re-use can produce important economies at no sacrifice to comfort or high visual impact.

Architects: Design Consortium
   1012 Marquette Avenue
   Minneapolis, Minnesota
   James Geisler, project architect
Owner: Roger Opp
Photographer: Phillip MacMillan James

MAIN LEVEL
5

LOWER LEVEL

MERCANTILE WHARF BUILDING

The Mercantile Wharf Building was not developed by one of Boston's poor communities. Nevertheless, it is linked to them.

Sharratt got the job to renovate the Mercantile Wharf Building by winning a developer/architect competition sponsored by the Boston Redevelopment Authority in 1972. The successful developer was Peabody Construction Company, which earlier built "Torre Unidad" for the elderly in Viviendas La Victoria in Boston's South End, designed by Sharratt. The excellent collaboration between Sharratt and Peabody led to their joint proposal.

The BRA had opposed Sharratt as "a troublemaker" during his early years as an advocacy planner. By 1972, however, leading officials of the BRA were calling the remodeled row houses of Viviendas La Victoria "the best residential rehabilitation in the city." And by the time Sharratt won the competition to rehabilitate the Mercantile Wharf Building, the BRA had begun recommending him to developers.

The BRA did no preliminary work on the building to get it ready for the developer. According to Sharratt: "it was full of dead animals, garbage, and rusted-out appliances—but it was very solid and well built." Originally designed in 1857 by Gridley James Fox Bryant in the French Second Empire Style, it once housed shipchandlers and sailmakers.

Sharratt's design preserves the original character of the building from the outside. Inside he has carved out a spectacular six-story atrium with a skylight extending its entire length. Two glass enclosed elevators descend to a pool.

The building contains 121 apartments ranging from duplexes and triplexes with lofts and skylights to one-bedroom apartments. Thirty-six of the apartment units are leased at market rents. Forty-two are for moderate-income and forty-three are low income. The subsidy program is HUD Section 707, and HUD Section 236.

MERCANTILE WHARF BUILDING, Boston, Massachusetts. Owner: *Mercantile Associates*. Architects: *John Sharratt Associates, Inc.—project architect: John Sharratt; project manager: Robert Meeker*. Consultants: *Engineers Design Group, Inc. (structural); William R. Ginns (mechanical); Sam Zax (electrical)*. General contractor: *Peabody Construction Co., Inc.*

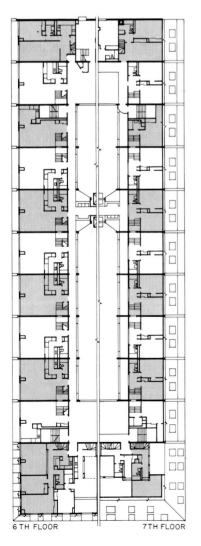

6 TH FLOOR   7TH FLOOR

WATERFRONT PARK   ATLANT

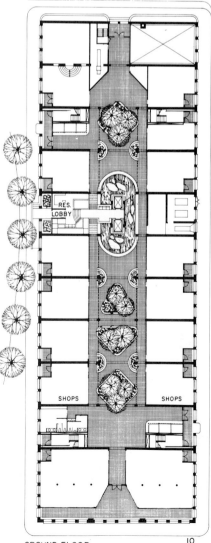

RES.
LOBBY

SHOPS   SHOPS

GROUND FLOOR   10

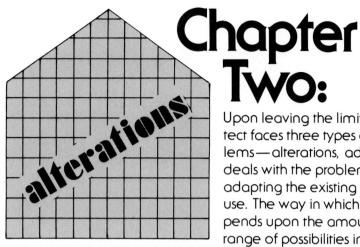

Chapter Two:

Upon leaving the limited scope of interiors, the architect faces three types of contextual design problems—alterations, additions, and in-fill. This chapter deals with the problem of alterations, the designer adapting the existing facade of the building to its new use. The way in which the facade is readapted depends upon the amount of modification involved. The range of possibilities includes reusing the facade essentially "as is," interweaving the old and new so that both are clearly visible, and overlaying dominant new elements upon the old facade.

The least radical alteration of a building facade is the least alteration. At times, the modification may be as minor as replacing small-paned windows with a single piece of glass. In other instances, the modifications may be more extensive, but the form of the original building remains essentially unchanged. An excellent example of this approach is the New York branch of the Bank of Tokyo (p. 44), in which the first-floor glazing was pulled back behind the existing attached columns to create a pedestrian walkway.

In the above example, the existing image clearly remains dominant. A slightly more radical appraoch combines new and old elements so that both are readily apparent. The new elements may be contained within the over-all mass of the original building, being primarily a two-dimensional alteration of the composition, or they may physically extend the original form. These new elements may be functional or they may be applied as ornament, strictly to make the old building more fashionable.

Fashion is the motivation for still more radical alterations in which new elements become the dominant part of the dialogue between past and present. Yet sensitively handled, the new elements enhance rather than outshout the old building—what matters is that the existing architecture remain a part of the conversation. The unforgivable occurs when the alteration obliterates the original, as exemplified by the ubiquitous 1950s metal screen or the more contemporary mirror glass applied directly over the existing facade.

In terms of scale, the alteration of an existing facade makes the least modification to a streetscape. To be sympathetic, such alterations must allow the original facade to continue to play a role in the new design. The relative importance of the new and existing elements is the variable that produces the range of solutions shown in the following examples.

Ezra Stoller © ESTO photos

BANK OF TOKYO

In searching for a solution to outmoded facilities with a dated appearance, this Manhattan bank found what was, for a commercial institution, a revolutionary new answer: stay in the existing building, preserve its visual assets of a grand facade and great public space, and replace its inadequate functional areas with sparkling new facilities —which give freshness to the whole project. Here is an example of good vision by the designers, good sense by the client, and good luck for the city.

Behind the "traditional" facade there is an almost-completely-new building, which is viewed first through a new recessed, ground-floor arcade (photo top). Within, the original central bay of the banking room has been surrounded by new construction. The central theme of the redesign is a sculpture by Isamu Noguchi.

There is general agreement among architects on the desirability of preservation and re-use of older buildings—not just of maintaining examples of architects' past efforts but to leave the valuable, varied context of the neighborhood intact. Too often, however, directors of corporations have thought that headquarters in older buildings were incompatible with the appearance of commercial efficiency, and they have moved from or torn down distinguished buildings primarily to obtain that desired "image." Thus. . . .

The newly remodeled Manhattan branch of the Bank of Tokyo is exceptional for two reasons. First, it clearly demonstrates that a sensitive remodeling—designed by Kajima International—can produce relatively inexpensive "new" space with not only a progressive image but a highly urbane and memorable image as well. Secondly, this project is distinguished in its respect for its environment: in its highly visible location across the street from the venerable Trinity Church Yard (foreground of bottom photo, previous page), the renovation has maintained the flavor of a uniquely "settled" neighborhood, and it has avoided the usual prolonged disruption of a new-construction site by producing the new space in a short time (during which—by planned staging—the tenants never left the building).

Essentially, Kajima's approach was to almost completely rebuild the interiors of 13 floors of the 22-floor building (designed by architect Bruce Price and built between 1894 and 1896) and to provide new glazing, elevators and mechanical systems for the remaining floors. Left intact, of course, was the structural frame,

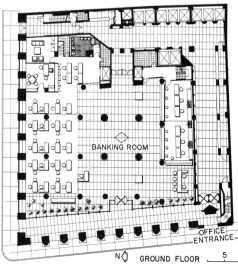

The designers have produced "a journey forward in time." The elevator lobby for the main floor (photo, above) is a white marble "funnel" leading through the original space to the starkly contemporary interiors on the floors above (photo, below).

the irreplaceable ornamented central bay of the banking room, the ceiling of the elevator lobby, and the elaborately carved stone facade. The crisp design of the new construction surrounding the central bay and on the floors above was designed in deliberate contrast to the richness and elaborations of the remaining original detail. And to accommodate and welcome the public at large, the frameless ground-floor glazing facing Trinity Church was pulled back to produce an inviting open arcade and a completely "modern" facade behind the original.

The design of the upper floors of the original building had largely been ignored in the original construction, and resembled the characterless spaces in many commercial buildings of the same vintage. Here, everything is new and appropriately appears that way. Each floor is entered via large elevator lobbies and reception areas, which provide an up-to-date spaciousness. New bronze-glass and metal window units are set in splayed recesses to reflect the natural light, while accommodating the two-foot wall thickness of the old facades.

THE BANK OF TOKYO, New York City. Client: The Bank of Tokyo. Designers: *Kajima International, Inc.— Nobutaka Ashihara, director; Ryozo Iwashiro, project designer; Martin Frauwirth, manager.* Associated architects: *Welton Becket Associates— Charles Ginste, project director.* Owner: *Sylvan Lawrence Company, Inc.—Fred Safran, architect to the owner.* Engineers: *Welton Becket Associates* (structural); *Lehr Associates* (mechanical/electrical). Consultants: *Donald Bliss* (lighting); *Carlos Ramirez & Albert Woods, Inc.* (graphics); *Frank N. Giampietro Associates Inc.* (kitchen); *Jerome Menell Company, Inc.* (audio-visual). General contractor: *Safran Builders, Inc.*

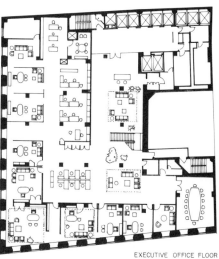

EXECUTIVE OFFICE FLOOR

The plan of an executive floor (opposite page) varies on a typical floor only by open work areas replacing the offices. An executive reception area is shown above, and an office at right. Paintings are by Asoma and Erica Kipp.

A restrained placement of furnishings and objects includes bright graphics in the cafeteria (photo, below). Exposed lighting in the office ceilings has slatted covers, and fixtures are designed to be at a-greater-than-normal distance apart with consequent energy savings. Floors in many parts of the offices and

reception areas are Tasmanian oak. The top photo shows the typical open office areas, and the photos at left show a mezzanine-level conference room (overlooking the banking floor) and a meeting room with audio-visual facilities.

TURTLE BAY TOWERS

Bill Rothschild photos except as noted

The renovation of a New York City office building into apartments has not only given a boost to inner-city housing but has done so in a luxurious manner, providing a quality of living space that can be an inducement for people to stay or move into the center city. Even though the building was not originally designed as an apartment complex, it can seriously compete with other luxury housing in the city because of its design amenities.

Constructed in 1929, this 24-story office building, located near the United Nations on Manhattan's East Side, was severely damaged by a gas explosion in 1974. The explosion funneled up the elevator shafts on the west side, blowing out a 50-foot-wide section of the brick facade from the street level to the top story, but structural damage was confined to the bank of elevators. The architects converted the service elevators to passenger use and cut away the demolished shafts and bent steel frame, leaving a V-shaped end wall (right). This provides a small street level courtyard and opens up the full 200-foot height of the west wall of apartments to natural light. This change also decreased the building's total volume, and zoning regulations permitted this "lost" space to be regained in the form of greenhouse-type windows installed on the exterior of most upper floors above the 17th level. Setbacks in the ziggurat building functionally permit the light to flow into the interiors while creating an attractive facade.

The interiors were designed to capitalize on views, light and spatial variety. A total of 341 apartments benefit from the commercial proportions of the building—12-foot-high ceilings, and 8-foot-high windows running the width of most apartments. Because setbacks occur on nearly every floor, and the need to comply with regulations set by the

The addition of greenhouses to the exterior is a major aspect of this conversion of office building to apartments. Each glass enclosure extends the apartment outward onto the terrace, and visually highlights the linear apartment design.

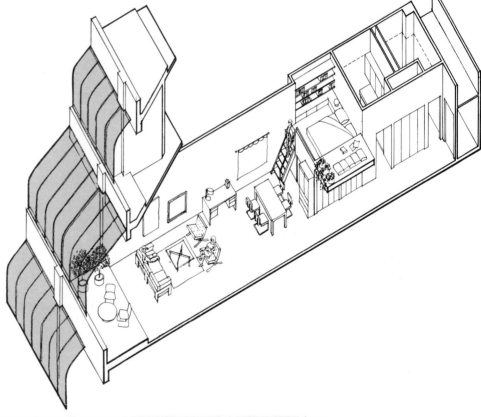

city's J-51 tax abatement program (which made this conversion possible) regarding the ratio of bedroom apartments to studios, each floor posed a separate planning problem. This was solved by the design of linear apartments (some 80 feet in length), running from the elevator core to the perimeter; kitchen and bath facilities that did not exist in the original were positioned near the central elevator core to simplify utilities. All the units are spacious, however, with the smallest studio 850 square feet.

An example of the creative utilization of the structure's idiosyncrasies is the redesign of the service elevators for passenger use. Because the cab platforms were larger than permitted by building codes, a glass-enclosed terrarium was located in the rear of each, providing an unexpected, yet pleasing experience.

The building's entrance was formerly the truck loading dock. Now multi-leveled (with a barrier-free access ramp) connecting a 100-foot-long lobby with elevators and street level entrance, it has been designed in a modern idiom but reminiscent of the building's 1929 origin.

The project was carried out under New York City's J-51 tax abatement program, which provides tax incentives for the conversion of commercial properties into residential use. It also has turned a serious disaster into a very successful asset.

TURTLE BAY TOWERS, New York, New York. Owner: *Rockrose Development Corporation*. Architects: *Bernard Rothzeid & Partners—Peter Thomson, partner-in-charge; Bernard Rothzeid and Carmi Bee, project designers; Vinod Devgan, job captain.* Engineers: *Harwood and Gould* (structural); *George Langer* (mechanical/electrical). Consultants: *Ranger Farrell Associates* (acoustical); *Nathan Silberman* (codes); *Soloman Sheer* (Board of Standard Appeals). Interior design: *Bernard Rothzeid & Partners—Marjorie Colt.* General contractor: *Rockrose Construction Corporation.*

TENTH FLOOR

FOURTH FLOOR

10

Lofts were included in the design of many apartments, especially studios, for they provide a spatial variety to the predominantly linear units. There are 341 apartments on the half-acre site, with configurations varying from studios to "townhouses" on the upper floors.

PENTHOUSE (LOWER FLOOR)

PENTHOUSE (UPPER FLOOR)

Susan Schwartz

THE LOGAN LEADER/THE NEWS DEMOCRAT

Happily fo the community of Russellville, Kentucky, the publisher of several local newspapers decided to expand his offices and printing plant in one of the few remaining nineteenth century buildings on the town square. The architects, Ryan, Cooke & Zuern, were asked to study the feasibility of recycling several sites on the square to provide current and future production space. Of some importance was the cleint's wish that the production of his publications be a visible part of the square's activity. The project was to include 7000 square feet of finished, air-conditioned, expandable space.

The selected location was a combined feed and hardware store that had endured the usual "modernizations." Its advantages—besides a prominent location on the square—included adjacent off-street parking, and a structure that offered positive separation of production and publication functions.

The street facade was stripped of years of various remodelings, revealing the original cast-iron and brick structure. These elements were restored and infilled with woodwork that duplicates the spirit of original doors and trim found stored in the cellar.

The two-story hardware store now houses the publications' editorial, circulation, advertising and management spaces, using an open-office design for immediate convertibility.

The one-story feed store was reworked to accommodate the pressroom and mailroom. Expansion of these two areas will occur in new space erected on the adjoining parking lot.

In the renovation, the existing masonry load-bearing structure could be used. The poplar floors of the feed store were removed and a new concrete slab poured on engineered fill for the presses. The floor boards and structural members were then reused for partition paneling and new stair construction. Plaster was removed from brick walls which were cleaned and left exposed. Existing wood floors and ceilings were simply cleaned, and new mechanical, electrical and sprinkler systems were installed throughout.

Outside, overhead utility lines and lighting were removed from the street facade, and the crumbling walk was replaced with new concrete and brick paving. Street trees were also added.

PRINTING PLANT AND OFFICE FOR THE LOGAN LEADER/THE NEWS DEMOCRAT, Russellville, Kentucky. Owner: *Logan Ink Inc.* Architects: *Ryan, Cooke and Zuern Associates Inc.* Contractor: *Logan Ink Inc.*

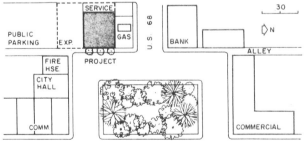

MECH.
DARK | CAMERA | TYPE
COMPOSITION
COMP. EXPAN.

SECOND FLOOR

One half of the second floor remains unassigned as expansion for the composition room and a self-contained news room. When this expansion occurs, the street floor will be reassigned for those business and administrative tasks directly involving the public.

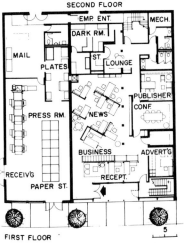

EMP. ENT. | MECH.
DARK RM.
MAIL | ST. | LOUNGE
PLATES
PUBLISHER
PRESS RM. | NEWS | CONF.
BUSINESS | ADVERT'G
RECEIV'G | RECEPT.
PAPER ST.

FIRST FLOOR   5

CARRIAGE HOUSE RENOVATION

A small turn-of-the-century carriage house has been transformed by architects Crissman & Solomon into a study and laboratory for its owner— and can serve as a self-sufficient guest house. Within the small building the architects have created an environment of great distinction and warmth.

The railing of the newly formed mezzanine is a continuous bookcase (see plans overleaf), which transforms the adjacent space into a reading gallery. The top of this bookcase serves as a useful ledge for plants and books as the photo (below) indicates, and also provides reference space. Opening off the reading gallery is the owner's study (left), with custom-built bookcases, files and a work ledge neatly fitted into the gambrel roof. From this study window the owner enjoys a magnificent view of the entire Boston skyline.

CARRIAGE HOUSE RENOVATION, Andover, Massachusetts. Owner: *Mr. and Mrs. John W. Kimball.* Architects: *Crissman & Solomon.* Structural engineer: *Eugene Hamilton.* Contractor: *Fitzgerald Henderson Porter Inc.*

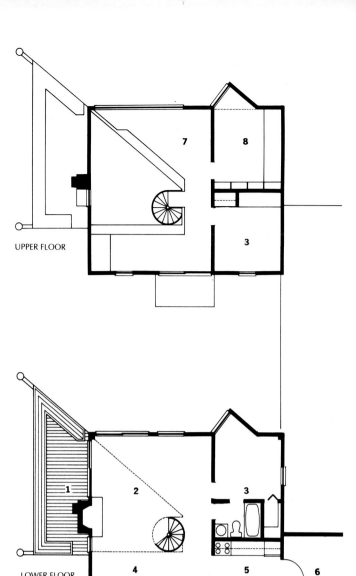

UPPER FLOOR

LOWER FLOOR

1 DECK
2 LIVING
3 BEDROOM
4 DINING
5 KITCHEN
6 BARN
7 READING GALLERY
8 STUDY

This renovated 60-year-old carriage house has been opened up to the west to afford its owners one of the most spectacular views in the greater Boston area. A very small building, only 25 by 30 feet, its lowest level is used as a garage and mechanical space. The main floor, which is at the same level as the barn floor with which it connects, has been transformed into a comfortable guest house with a living-dining area, a bedroom and a kitchen.

The second floor has become a mezzanine through the subtraction of a wedge-shaped portion. This judicious paring away adds to the volumetric complexity of the living-dining area, affording views upward to the roof and from the mezzanine downward to the main floor.

This solution was made practical by the existence of a solid wood beam, approximately 8 by 10 inches, which bisects the structure in the east-west direction and supports the second floor. It serves as the anchor for one end of the steel rod that became the necessary means of tying the south wall to the rest of the structure after the wedge-shaped portion of the floor had been removed. A vertical tie rod from which this beam is hung is part of the old structure and is connected to the trusses of the gambrel roof. Both the horizontal and vertical rods can be seen in the photographs opposite. The location of this beam determined the placement of the circular stair which ties into it at the second floor landing.

The old wood flooring which was removed was used for patching in the renovated areas. All the finished wood floors are made up of the old planks.

As the plans indicate, the south and west elevations were opened up as much as possible with the two-story living space and deck facing the view, and the smaller spaces arranged along the barn side of the building. The major view is captured from the study and the first floor bedroom by means of the angled windows which project from the west facade. The entire building was reclad in cedar shingles, except for the roof, which had been asphalt-shingled before the restoration.

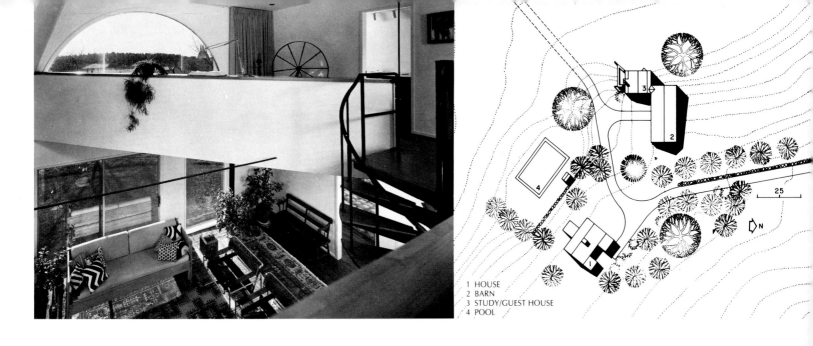

1 HOUSE
2 BARN
3 STUDY/GUEST HOUSE
4 POOL

59

REMODELING OF STANFORD SHOPPING CENTER

Architects Bull Field Volkmann Stockwell used a theatrical approach to modernize the outmoded Stanford Shopping Center in Palo Alto, California. Much of the work is like a stage-set design, creating not just a new facade but a new and festive atmosphere. Underlying such devices as new loggias, arches, outdoor display areas and graphics—all interconnected by an unusual framework system of bent pipe—is a new and ordered spatial development, enhanced by lush landscaping. It offers the retailer marketing flexibility while providing a vibrant and lively environment for the shopper where there was none before.

Gary Wincott

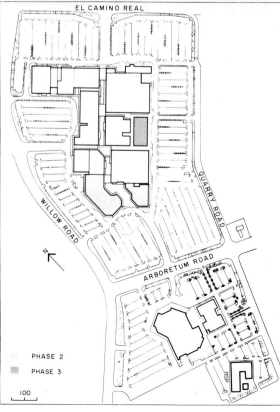

EL CAMINO REAL

WILLOW ROAD

QUARRY ROAD

ARBORETUM ROAD

PHASE 2
PHASE 3

100

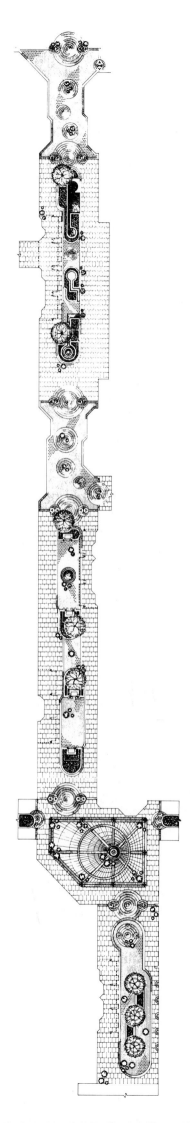

The remodeling and new construction of the Stanford Shopping Center (owned by and located near Stanford University) was done in three phases. The design problem was clear: how to turn a 1950s-style shopping complex into an attractive, unified whole with renewed vitality; maintaining the existing structures and the linear mall, while creating new retail space. The architect's solution was to de-emphasize the multi-form structures, using them as a back-drop, and to center remodeling efforts on the 900-foot-long mall.

"The design concept was to create a sequence of spaces—a parade with a strong cadence and ceremony," explains John Field, architect-in-charge. It is this sequential experience highlighted by an incredible but integrated array of forms—in arches, loggias, fountains, awnings, landscaping and lighting—that have altered the entire atmosphere of the mall.

The main design device used to articulate the spaces and modulate the visual experiences is a dramatic change in scale from one area to another—producing a sequence of grand- and intimately-scaled forms and spaces. The visitor rambles in and out of covered pathways along varying widths of the mall, around rusticated modern columns, landscaping, fountains and sitting areas, through the large volume of pavilion display space, and continually through arches formed from a bent-pipe framework system. The arches separate the different sections, and echo the Romanesque arches prevalent in the architecture of Stanford University. There is a further deliberate attempt to focus the shopper's attention on display windows by limiting the over-all background color scheme to muted colors; and yet by the positioning of arches directing views into other areas, the shopper is subtly enticed to continue moving to experience what's ahead.

REMODELING OF STANFORD SHOPPING CENTER, Palo Alto, California. Architects: *Bull Field Volkmann Stockwell—John Louis Field, architect-in-charge; Sherwood Stockwell, master plan architect; David L. Paoli, project architect; Daniel Chung, Gary Fong and Paul J. Meade, project director.* Engineers: *L. F. Robinson & Associates* (structural), *Cooper Clark & Associates* (foundation), *Gayner Engineers* (mechanical/electrical), *Brian Kangas Foulk & Associates* (civil). Consultants: *John Smith* (shopping center advisor), *Frank Henry and Associates* (project manager for Stanford University), *Charles M. Salter* (acoustical), *William Lam Associates Inc.* (lighting), *Fire Protection Engineers* (fire protection), *Reis & Company and Intrinsics* (graphic design), *Clyde Winters* (graphic fabrication coordinator), *Peter Adamson* (cost). Landscape architects: *Fong & Larocca Associates.* General contractor: *Rudolph & Sletten.*

The shopping center, as designed in the 1950s (left and right), was laid out with a linear mall surrounded by four large anchor stores. The redesign makes much more of the mall with semi-circular loggias, covered with bronze-colored acrylic plastic replacing corrugated aluminum walkway covers. Each loggia is lined with lights every 10 feet adding a sparkling quality at night. With the buildings painted muted tan and white colors, the only splash of color is in the banners hung from the loggias. These banners also break the long, linear view under the walkways.

John Field   *John Field*

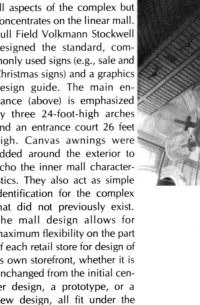

The redesign of the Stanford Shopping Center encompasses all aspects of the complex but concentrates on the linear mall. Bull Field Volkmann Stockwell designed the standard, commonly used signs (e.g., sale and Christmas signs) and a graphics design guide. The main entrance (above) is emphasized by three 24-foot-high arches and an entrance court 26 feet high. Canvas awnings were added around the exterior to echo the inner mall characteristics. They also act as simple identification for the complex that did not previously exist. The mall design allows for maximum flexibility on the part of each retail store for design of its own storefront, whether it is unchanged from the initial center design, a prototype, or a new design, all fit under the loggia. In some instances, where there are large blank walls as a result of the initial plan, small specialty shops can be designed to fill the space without disturbing the circulation patterns. One clothing store (below left) is designed by the architects. The pavilion is a new space created specifically for outdoor displays. It is here that the only structural alteration occurs (original space shown in photo bottom right, page 62). The "grandness" of the columns results from the welding together into a cluster the pipes identical to those used throughout the center.

Gary Wincott

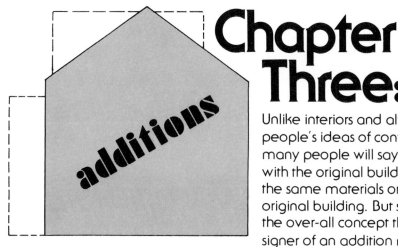

Chapter Three:

Unlike interiors and alterations, additions typify most people's ideas of contextual design. When asked, many people will say that an addition is in harmony with the original building because the new wing uses the same materials or continues the roof line of the original building. But such devices merely implement the over-all concept that unites new and old. The designer of an addition must select a concept that achieves this goal while simultaneously accommodating the new space. Conceptually, the addition may be a reproduction of the original building, an abstraction of it, a background building, or a sympathetic contrast to the original building.

Reproduction may seem the easiest choice, but one that is not as easy as it seems. As Hugh Newell Jacobsen's Victorian addition (p. 66) shows, simply choosing to continue the style of the original building does not eliminate the task of designing the exterior of the addition. Reproduction is more than copying. Instead, the designer must thoroughly understand the stylistic language of the original building to be able to reassemble the parts around the new space. Without this understanding, imitation originally intended as flattery becomes parody. However, even if the designer has the ability and courage to dress his creation in the fashion of its predecessor, producing the garments can still be problematic. Materials that once were common are often extremely expensive or even unobtainable now, and long-forgotten details clumsily executed can fatally mar the concept. Yet when done well, reproduction can be smart dress indeed.

A slightly less deferential concept often used for additions is the abstraction of the original building. The intent is to achieve harmony between the old and new by recreating the essence of the original building without reproducing it in toto. Generally this is handled by designing an addition with massing similar to the original building but substituting contemporary details. The shortcoming of this concept is often the failure to recognize the importance of ornament. Even when the addition imitates the massing of the existing building, the loss of ornament can change the scale completely. Even so, abstraction is a valid concept for additions that are both properly deferential, yet thoroughly contemporary.

Proper deference to the contemporary idiom can also be achieved by focusing the viewer's attention on the existing building and providing the additional space in the least obtrusive manner; the addition becomes a "background" building. Focusing attention is especially effective when the addition is sufficiently larger than the original building and literally becomes a background against which the principal object is viewed.

Although paradoxical, another conceptual approach for sympathetically adding onto an existing building is to contrast the new with the old. As previously discussed, sympathetic contrast increases the appreciation of both architectural styles. In the case of additions, the contrast is often between the solidness of the masonry walls of the historic building and the transparency of the glass-and-steel skin of the addition. The Florence Museum of Modern Art (p. 83) and the East Cambridge Savings Bank (p. 86) exemplify this approach. But as the Mayers & Schiff residential addition shows (p. 96), equally revealing juxtapositions can be created by other devices.

Adding to an existing building is the most recognized contextual design problem. By its very nature, such a problem imposes considerable constraints upon the designer. Yet within these constraints, he retains the choice of complete deference to the existing building through reproduction; partial deference; or sympathetic contrast. Properly executed, all these concepts can produce dazzling results.

RESIDENTIAL REMODELING AND ADDITION

Few readers will recognize Hugh Jacobsen's touch in the exterior of this remodeled Victorian house in a suburb of Washington, D.C. The original portion of this house was built in 1871 as an outbuilding to a larger house of similar style. The main house was long ago erased by a change in the street plan, but the small house remained, surviving several owners and a series of modest alterations.

When the present owner purchased the property in 1975, Hugh Jacobsen was retained to make a new addition and to thoroughly modernize the interiors. But because the neighborhood was old, the corner site prominent, and the Victorian character of the design so lovingly preserved through earlier alterations, Jacobsen carried out the new exterior work using the old mold—or carefully studied reproductions of that mold. The original entry with its covered porch was removed. A floor-to-ceiling bay window was substituted and then repeated on the new wing. Window trim, fenestration and eave details were carefully researched as were paint colors used in small country houses of the 1870s. Both in the old exterior and in the addition, the ethos of the earlier era was preserved, including the promise of well proportioned, carefully developed spaces within.

On the inside, however, the Old Queen would not have found herself at home. The house is fully air conditioned and the interior development of the spaces, their arrangement, their furnishing are pure Jacobsenian. Starting with the glass entry link, and continuing across two floors, the house is contemporary and equipped with all the appurtenances of modern life.

There is always a special feeling about houses in which the old and the new are beautifully harmonized. Here this harmony is achieved very purposefully through a process of historical allusion that, as recently as five years ago, might have been unthinkable for most architects and even today takes courage and sensitivity.

Architect: Hugh Newell Jacobsen
 1427 27th Street, N.W.
 Washington, D.C.
Engineer:
 Kraas & Mok (structural)
Contractor: Owner
Photographer: Robert Lautman
 Courtesy of House & Garden © 1977,
 Coude-Nast Publications, Inc.

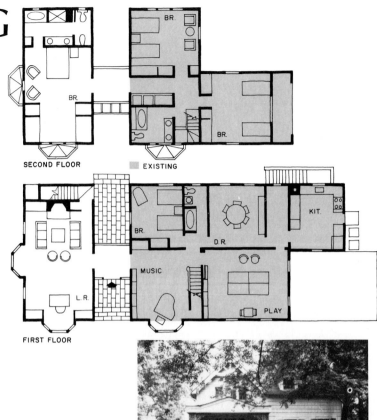

SECOND FLOOR   ▨ EXISTING

FIRST FLOOR

The small photo (above) shows the original portion of the small house. The entrance, across a porch, leads into what is now the music room (photo lower right). The living room (photo below) and bedroom above make up the new addition.

John L. Alexandrowicz

SARAH SCAIFE GALLERY

An initial mandate for Edward Larrabee Barnes' design for the Sarah Scaife Gallery at the Carnegie Institute in Pittsburgh was that there be an abundant supply of pellucid natural light to illuminate the gallery's paintings. The paintings—first-rate Impressionist, Post-Impressionist and American works, plus what director Leon Arkus calls a "spotty" collection from other periods—are a part of a museum of art, which is in turn (with a library, music hall and museum of natural history) a part of the cultural institution founded in Pittsburgh in 1890 by Andrew Carnegie.

Dick Behl, Associated Photographers, Inc.

Barnes' Scaife Gallery is an addition in several senses—physically it is an addition to an existing building, first built in 1895 and then greatly enlarged in 1907. More generally, though, the new building is an addition to a public institution of mixed use and considerable tradition. So the design task (in addition to providing good natural light for the paintings) was to make the new building well integrated with the old one—caring, for instance, for the modulation between the new galleries and the existing ones, and for the way the stark facade of the addition meets the more softly articulated (but bigger) Carnegie facade.

Two faces

Scaife Gallery has two main entrances (above and left), one of them facing the street, though set back from it,

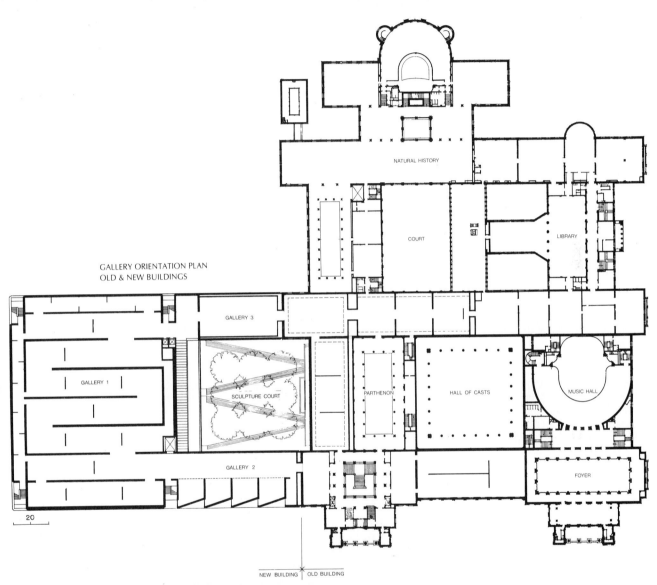

GALLERY ORIENTATION PLAN
OLD & NEW BUILDINGS

NATURAL HISTORY

COURT

LIBRARY

GALLERY 3

GALLERY 1

SCULPTURE COURT

PARTHENON

HALL OF CASTS

MUSIC HALL

GALLERY 2

FOYER

20

NEW BUILDING | OLD BUILDING

Ronald A. Layport photos

Much of the plan form of the Scaife Gallery is generated by the older Carnegie Institute to which it is joined. The two wings that surround the courtyard are extensions of protrusions on the older building, and the square plan of the courtyard itself recalls the square Hall of Casts inside the Carnegie building. The rectangular mass of the main part of the new building expansively suggests a third pavilion to complement the two Beaux Arts ones next door. The photograph on the left shows the fountains just outside the street-side entrance.

and echoing something of the formality of the older Carnegie Institute building. The second entrance, which is on the other side of the building and a full level below on the sloping site, opens onto a vehicular access road and, beyond that, to terraced parking lots that can accommodate up to 320 cars. From this entrance, the visitor moves directly into the gallery's courtyard (plans right), which steps gently back upwards to the level of the street entrance, and which is embellished with a waterfall, trees and, of course, works of sculpture from the museum's collection. On two sides the courtyard is flanked by glass-walled promenades (which also double as galleries), and from one of these a massive stone staircase leads upward still farther to the main gallery spaces.

In form the building is a rectilinear mass two stories high on the front and three on the back, with two wings that embrace the courtyard and connect to the existing Carnegie Institute building. On the lowest level (not shown in the adjacent plans, and accessible only from the back side of the building) are a small auditorium, a children's room and rooms for storage and for mechanical equipment. On the main level are the street entrance lobby, a small cafe, a museum shop, more storage and administrative offices and workrooms. Above this level are the main galleries.

Up to the galleries

Having all of the main gallery spaces on the top floor of the new building obviously provides the chance to achieve ideal natural lighting in them, and, as importantly, it puts them on the same level as the existing galleries in the Carnegie Institute. In a three-story building, however, it also results in a relatively small amount of the building's total floor area being devoted to gallery

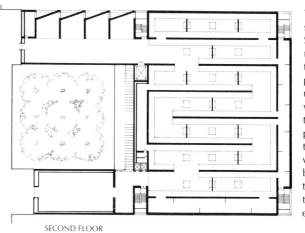

SECOND FLOOR

The photograph on the right shows the courtyard of the Scaife Gallery seen from underneath the main stairway leading to the upper floor. The suspended glass wall system is made of ½-inch tempered glass with ¾-inch tempered glass fins to provide wind bracing in place of mullions. The photograph below shows the stairway from the street side of the building, looking back through the courtyard. Stone cladding is thermal finish Norwegian emerald pearl granite.

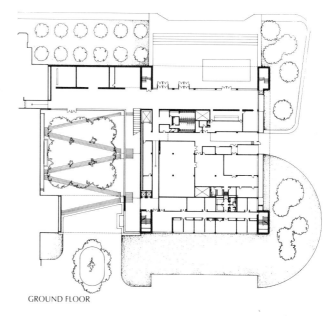

GROUND FLOOR

John L. Alexandrowicz

The section through the Scaife Gallery on the right shows the natural lighting system in the galleries on the top floor. Daylight enters through skylights on the roof and passes first through a set of horizontal diffusing glass panels and then through a second, vertical set into the gallery space. The pyramidal skylights above the suspended panels are also diffusers above panels that can be removed to admit light straight down onto a piece of sculpture. The artificial lights seen in the photograph above provide substitute light at the same angle as daylight.

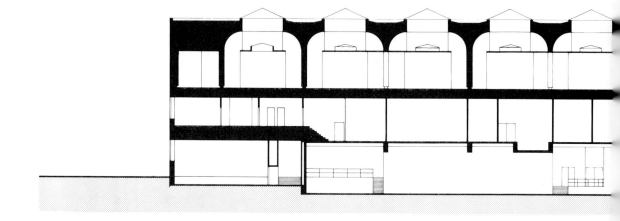

John L. Alexandrowicz

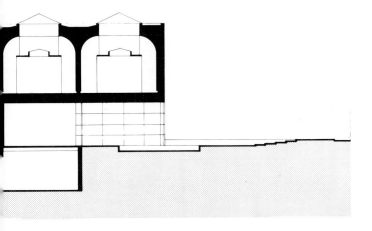

space—a phenomenon which, according to the architects, caused no rancor here because of the need for a number of non-gallery rooms in the building, including generous storage and workrooms that serve the older galleries as well as the new ones.

In plan, the new galleries are a series of interlocking U's and demi-U's on which works from the Scaife's permanent collection are displayed. Smaller, more self-contained exhibition areas flank these main gallery spaces on three sides. In connecting the new galleries to the old ones, Barnes has developed an even and unjarring choreography—albeit one that encourages (and almost demands) a linear pilgrimage by the visitor.

Light on white

In the Scaife Gallery, says Leon Arkus, there are "no intrusive artifices of architecture. The art comes forward unembellished, with all the life the artist gave it." And, according to Barnes, "the second floor—white space with soft modulated daylight—turns all attention to the paintings." Thus the director and the architect of the Scaife articulate the prevailing contemporary view of how art should be displayed: with as little intrusion as possible from the surrounding environment. (This view, it is worth noting, stands in contrast to the centuries-old custom of hanging paintings on colored and textured walls in elaborate architectural spaces, and Barnes himself points out that the Modern penchant for white walls suits some paintings, like Impressionist ones, better than others, like somber Old Masters.) The Scaife Gallery follows the non-intrusive Modern persuasion, but elegantly varies and enlivens it with a soft and even shower of natural light that enters through skylights, passes through two diffusers and then bounces from vaults that spring from the walls where the paintings are hung—providing the greatest level of intensity there (in contrast to the usual skylit gallery, where the ceiling is brightest), and subtly changing in color with the hour of day and with the seasons.

SARAH SCAIFE GALLERY, Carnegie Institute, Pittsburgh, Pennsylvania. Architect: *Edward Larrabee Barnes—associate-in-charge: Percy K. Keck; project architect: Armand P. Avakian.* Engineers: *Severud Associates* (structural); *Swindell-Dressler Company* (civil); *Joseph R. Loring and Associates, Inc.* (mechanical and electrical). Consultants: *Bolt, Beranek and Newman, Inc.* (acoustical); *Donald L. Bliss* (lighting); *Mary Barnes and Paul Planert Design Associates, Inc.* (interiors); *Dan Kiley and Partners* (landscape); *Dimianos and Pedone* (graphics); *Turner Construction Company* (cost). General contractor: *Turner Construction Company.*

Ronald A. Layport

PARK-DANFORTH HOME FOR THE ELDERLY

When the Home For Aged Men in Portland, Maine, was ready to expand, it could have torn down the fine old residence it was utilizing, and started over. The house was in adequate condition, but it violated many of the more stringent code requirements developed over the last 10 years for this kind of housing, and needed to be completely "modernized." But it was not torn down; it was saved and used as the esthetic keystone for further development of the property, as the photograph at right so nicely shows. Now both the old home and the major new addition that it generated are housing elderly people, and maintaining the architectural continuity of the 18th-century residential neighborhood around them. And the people of Portland, Maine are publicly praising both the sponsor and their architect, as they should.

The old Levi Cutter House, built ca. 1810, with extensions added during the 19th century, was placed in trust by Mr. Cutter when he died to be converted to a home for elderly men. It remained in this use until 1964, housing from six to 24 men in a kind of boarding house arrangement. Then the board of directors of the trust decided they should try to enlarge the effectiveness of the home, and hired the young firm of Bruce Porter Arneill as their architects. Arneill studied the problem, and came up with the solution on these pages. As Arneill puts it: "The basic concept was to have the old and new buildings complement each other, and the space be-

The three plans below show the major floors of the housing complex, and the grading, with the previously existing facilities overlaid in color. The long neck linking the two parts allows a clear division between the two, creates an adequate space for an entrance vestibule, and allows the corridor to slope up or down to meet existing floor heights. The original house, it is apparent, had several additions to it between 1810 and 1900.

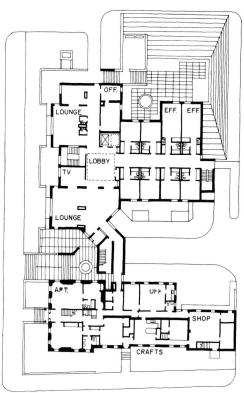

FIRST FLOOR

10

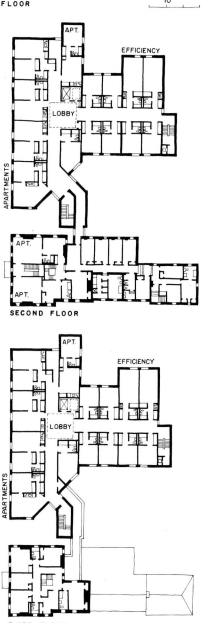

SECOND FLOOR

THIRD FLOOR

Bill Maris photos

The west end of the new addition (below) is designed so that the corridor on each level can plug into a future addition, and the new elevatoring and kitchen system has been designed to accommodate this future addition, too. Below, the interior of the new lounge looks onto the street, and some of the other early 19th century architecture of the neighborhood. At right, the new main entrance of the home fits between the old and new buildings. Note how the major horizontal elements of each facade line up with each other.

tween invite you in. . . . We studied all the pertinent characteristics of the older building, and these influenced the detail design decisions on our new work."

The first problem of designing a compatible addition was one of scale: the finished new facility was to house 85 people, both men and women, rather than the six people it had housed for the last few years, so it would have been easy to dominate the old house with the new addition. The problem was solved by maintaining the roof line of the house, by making the windows in the new addition about the same size as the old window shapes (including the shutters) and by matching the old brick as closely as possible. The mansard roof of the addition allows a fourth floor to be worked in while still maintaining a three-floor roof line.

Matching the floor elevations in the old house was a problem, because new construction generally requires a greater floor-to-floor height than the nine feet of the original building. The nine foot height was accomplished by using brick bearing wall construction, concrete planking for the floors, and by eliminating dropped and suspended ceilings except in certain corridors. The interior ceiling height is still maintained from eight feet to eight feet six inches throughout. The front facade of the new addition is in exactly the same plane as the facade of the house, and about three times as long, but the undercutting for terraces and porches that occurs at the ground floor of the addition lightens its mass effectively. Because the addition went up four stories, large parts of the site became available for terracing and exterior use (photo, above right) that would not have been available if an earlier two-story concept had been continued.

The old stairway of the original house is intact inside, as well as most of its original moldings. What the architect has added is paint; paint in bright colors and broad stripes to give the interior of the house a fresh new life without permanently harming any of its old forms. The house and its earlier additions now provide sleeping rooms for 22 people, plus activity and storage areas. The new addition houses the kitchen, dining room, administrative offices, lounges, and 15 one-bedroom apartments, eight efficiency apartments, and 27 single rooms.

The main entrance to both the old and the new parts of the complex is now between the two structures, shown in the large photo, opposite. The steps here are fewer than in the old entrance, and because of the grading of the site a person can avoid all steps into the building from the parking area at the rear.

The Park-Danforth Home has room sizes that are substantially larger than the FHA standards for elderly housing. There is no Federal money at all in the project; the original trust itself put up about half the funds and local Portland banks put up the other half.

PARK-DANFORTH HOME FOR THE ELDERLY, Portland, Maine. Architect: *Bruce Porter Arneill;* structural engineer: *Rudolph Besier;* mechanical engineers: *Francis Associates;* interior design: *Raymond Doernberg;* contractor: *Consolidated Constructors & Builders, Inc.*

TEKNOR APEX COMPANY OFFICES

Central Avenue in Pawtucket, Rhode Island (photo left) is scarcely a dream site. Run-down at the heels, with some 19th century factory buildings mixed with cheap-as-possible cinder block warehouse space, some stores from the last era when glass block was groovy and lots of parking lots, it is—alas —typical of just-outside-downtown in a hundred American cities.

Teknor Apex's program for the remodeling of its Central Avenue corporate offices was similarly modest. The need was for new office space—"utilitarian, inexpensive, nothing ostentatious"; and since the company produces products only for resale to other manufacturers, "concerns regarding public image are limited," as indeed they are often in the plans of industry for its building projects.

Says architect Warren Platner: "We rather enjoy the task of trying to make something of distinction from very little, especially if there is something inherited to respect."

The starting point for the remodeling was: 1. The 19th-century factory building shown below—which behind patched-on exhaust ducts and decades of grime did offer "something inherited to respect" in its old brick, arched windows, and New England forthrightness, and . . . 2. The completely featureless cinder block structure next door (see "before" photo on

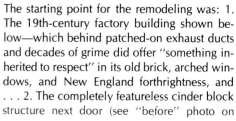

page 78) which adjoined the plant, was owned by the client, and had been used as a discount retail outlet.

Until the remodeling, Teknor Apex's office space had been contained in the factory building, and a need for more production space and more office space led to the job.

Platner's solution to the space problem was to remodel the cinder block building for general office space (top of plan) and add a small, one-story addition beyond for executive offices (bottom of plan) which opens through an all-glass wall (photo below) to a tree-shaded court. The planning of the new offices was, of course, a fairly routine design problem. What is not routine is the totally new character of space and environment and order created by Platner and his design team.

The cinder block building (top photo, preceding page), to be used for general office space, was given new windows (simply punched through the cinder block walls and given the arch form borrowed from the plant) and refaced in brick matched as closely as posible to the factory. The brick chosen was an inexpensive common brick made by the same producer who provided the brick for the plant nearly 100 years ago.

The unsightly yard between the plant and the office building (preceding page) was landscaped and semi-enclosed with the arched wall shown in the photos. This provided a handsome new entry court for the plant employees.

As the top photo shows, the wall continues at the lower level of the new executive-office wing, extends past to form the arched entry to the main entrance (both bottom photos) and terminates in a freestanding wall at the property line. This second larger court is paved in matching blocks and planted with plane trees and euonymus. Platner's conscious decision (with the client's approval) to open this courtyard to the neighborhood was accepted by the neighborhood: it is now a busy and appreciated mid-block passage. The reflective-glass curtain wall assures privacy for company executives while giving them a pleasant and controlled view—and doubling the apparent size of the court.

The buttressed brick wall at the right in the photo below is freestanding, simply separating the courtyard from the not-too-handsome commercial buildings beyond.

The interiors are simple and spartan, and of common and inexpensive materials, but—as is characteristic of Platner's work—detailed with great care and precision. In the remodeled section (photos below and page 82) the retail-store space (''before'' photo at left) was stripped to its wood structure and concrete floor. The multitude of columns in the space was mostly incorporated in new partitions, which are framed and trimmed in red oak, and are about half clear glass and half pre-finished hardboard with a random-groove pattern. Conference-room spaces are glass-enclosed, but have narrow-slat blinds which can be lowered for privacy when needed. Carpeting is on-slab, and the ceiling is a conventional hung ceiling with ''the least expensive lighting fixture made by the manufacturer. We like the fixture,''

Platner says, ''because being the cheapest, it was also the plainest and simplest.'' About 50 per cent of the furniture was moved from the old office and repainted to match new steel furniture designed for the manufacturer by Platner some years ago.

In the new executive-office space, the same simple finishes were used, though, of course, spaces are more generous and the furniture more luxurious (mostly wood—and again designed for the manufacturers by the architect). As the top photos at right show, most of these offices share the view of the entry courtyard, but have narrow-slat blinds because the space faces west. In the entry lobby (top right) a skylight and a panel of wood parquet are intended to create ''a sense of location.''

Construction of this new space is (to save

money) short span, with columns of square steel tubing and light weight trusses. But again Platner achieved some elegance with such simple devices as incandescent wall-washers and a foot-wide strip of parquet as a border around the carpet.

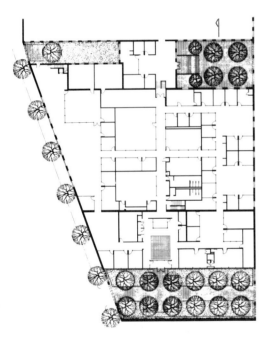

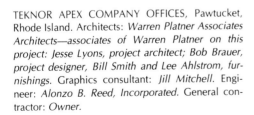

TEKNOR APEX COMPANY OFFICES, Pawtucket, Rhode Island. Architects: *Warren Platner Associates Architects—associates of Warren Platner on this project: Jesse Lyons, project architect; Bob Brauer, project designer, Bill Smith and Lee Ahlstrom, furnishings.* Graphics consultant: *Jill Mitchell.* Engineer: *Alonzo B. Reed, Incorporated.* General contractor: *Owner.*

VILLA STROZZI
MUSEUM

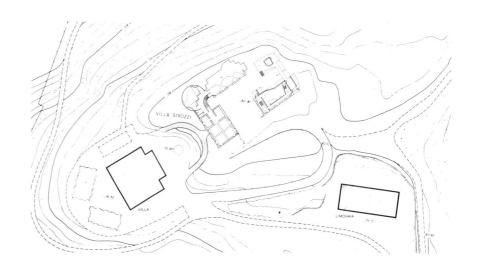

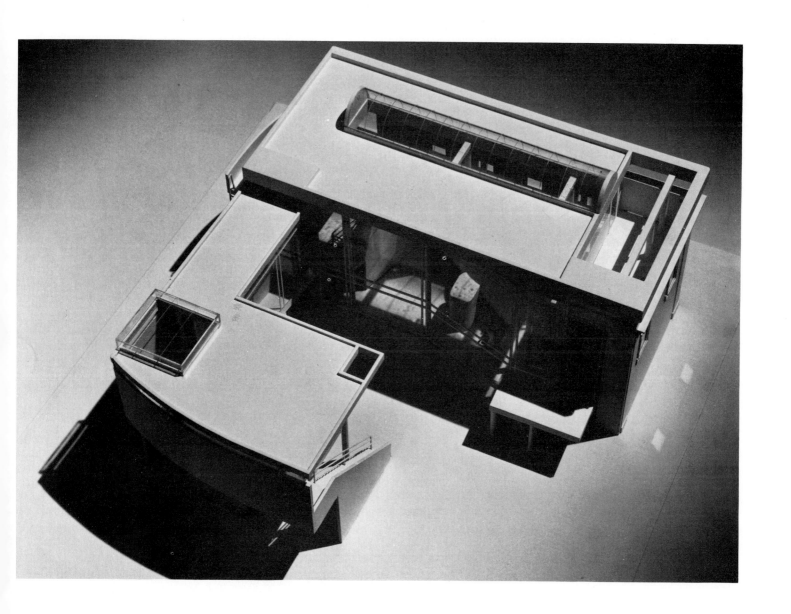

One of the more unusual projects in Richard Meier's (or anyone's) office is this Museum of Modern Art for the City of Florence, Italy. It is planned in a way that may make strict preservationists shudder—but it is completely within the new spirit of building modern facilities that respect the visual richness provided by older buildings. There is to be a whole new architectural entity here, incorporating two existing walls of the stables of the 19th century Villa Strozzi. The old walls will visually tie the new building to a nearby structure, which is being restored by architect Hans Hollein, and will respect the existing relationship of the stable to the courtyard and courtyard-approach views (see site plan left).

Tradition is respected without fakery—illustrating that the best of the old and new can be integral, when there is something of value left with which to start. As can be seen in the photo of the existing building (opposite, top), the walls to be saved were regarded by Meier as they were by the original Villa architect, Guiseppe Poggi, as an independently important part of the original structure—for Poggi, a screen to hide the lesser building behind. Meier has taken great care to match his new materials to those of the original building, which was constructed of a dark gray stone (and later covered with stucco, which will be removed in the new work).

The Museum is to be a carefully articulated frame for the older walls, which are presented as sculpture. At the same time, the walls provide an anchoring solid mass, against which Meier has always generated his freely flowing public spaces. The heavy wall itself takes the place in the composition of strongly defined spaces. The visitor passes through (or in this case, around) a confining introduction to the spatial drama beyond. The main room of the museum is to be a multilevel space, connected by ramps (between the second and third levels) to a remote exhibition space (lower level in the model, overleaf). Visitors will be confronted with far more visual interest than the paintings on the walls: alternating solid and transparent wall-planes will provide surprise views of Florence in the distance, as well as of the exhibition hall, all from various elevations and angles. The two separate building volumes will provide additional views toward and into each other.

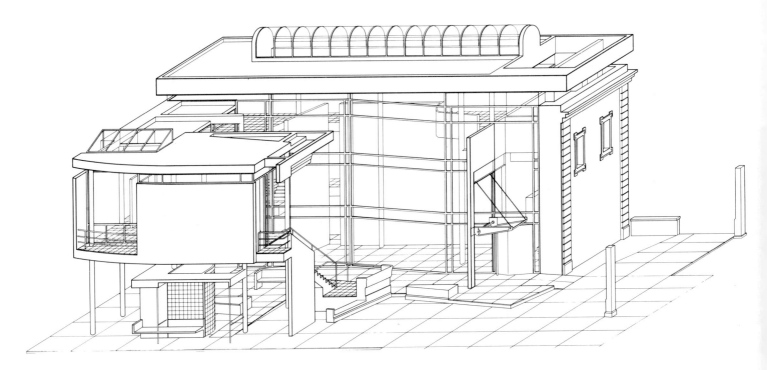

Contained within two existing walls of a stable, this new exhibition gallery will have spiraling-loop circulation between the balcony levels in the main hall and the floor of the secondary gallery. The latter is projected from the large building to form an enclosure for the adjacent courtyard (see site plan, preceding page, top). It is reached by a ramp, in a connecting neck, from the second level of the main room. Another sloped ramp, located alongside, leads visitors to the top balcony in the main room and the end of the circuit. Much of the light will be natural, introduced by skylights and the glass walls, most of which face north. The structure is steel with a rectangular grid of round columns that belies the planned visual complexity, and gives a light-weight appearance, in contrast to the visual weight of the existing walls.

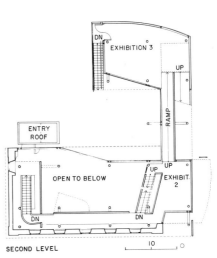

SECOND LEVEL

Existing building and models for new
structure showing relationship of walls
and courtyard.

VILLA STROZZI MUSEUM, for Florence, Italy.
Architect: *Richard Meier*.

Louis Checkman

SHERMAN FAIRCHILD PHYSICAL SCIENCES CENTER

According to Jean Paul Carlhian, the design objective of this new glass and concrete tower is to give new life to an entire college science complex, by linking a new laboratory building (now under construction) with the existing physics and chemistry buildings.

The tower gives physical expression to Dartmouth College's desire to reinforce the functional interaction between the scientific disciplines. This linkage problem was a complicated one, requiring ingenuity on the part of the architects in solving the geometric incompatibility and non-corresponding floor levels of the existing buildings. The tower link will accommodate a fourth wing (see plan), which may be added in the future.

·As conceived and built, the new link is a concrete tower based geometrically on two triangles, creating a strong new diagonal axis at the very focus of the science complex. This central space, formed by the adjoining buildings and walls of glass, provides access and primary vertical circulation to the entire science center. In addition to serving as a circulatory node, the new link also acts as a mini-commons, with sitting areas on each floor and a variety of artistic and scientific displays. At the tower base is a new entrance for the entire complex.

The older physics building has been remodeled, and the existing chemistry building has also been recycled. The new laboratory wing under construction is being built according to the SEF system. Barely discernible in the upper left hand corner of the bird's-eye photo (opposite page), it embodies a sophisticated modular vocabulary developed jointly by the Toronto School System and the Ford Foundation.

A full complement of sub-systems is being used, including pre-finished wall panels, electric-electronic components and demountable interior walls with excellent STC ratings. The space enclosed is extremely flexible. The architects believe it to be the most ambitious application of industrialized architecture so far attempted in New England.

SHERMAN FAIRCHILD PHYSICAL SCIENCES CENTER, Dartmouth College, Hanover, New Hampshire. Architects: *Shepley Bulfinch Richardson & Abbott.* Engineers: *Nichols, Norton and Zaldastani, Inc.* (structural); *Leo J. Crowley Associates, Inc.* (mechanical); *Thompson Engineering Co., Inc.* (electrical); *William Cavanaugh* (acoustics). General contractor: *Jackson Construction Company.*

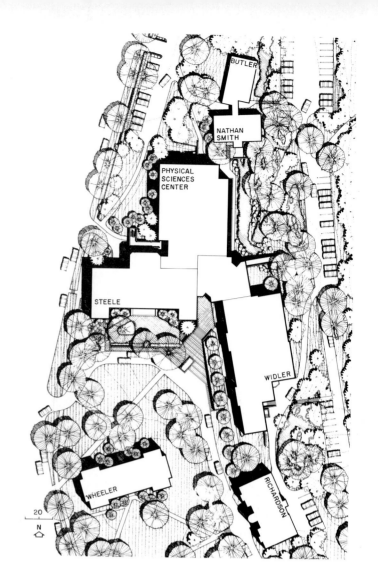

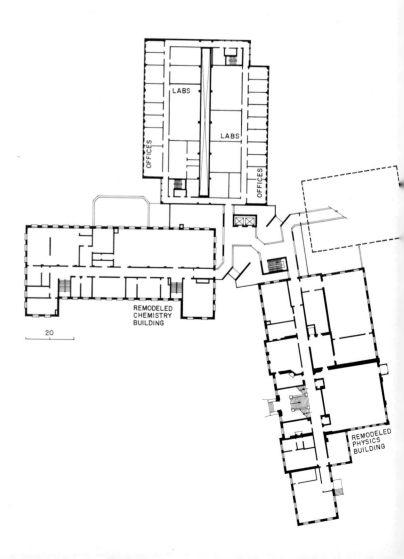

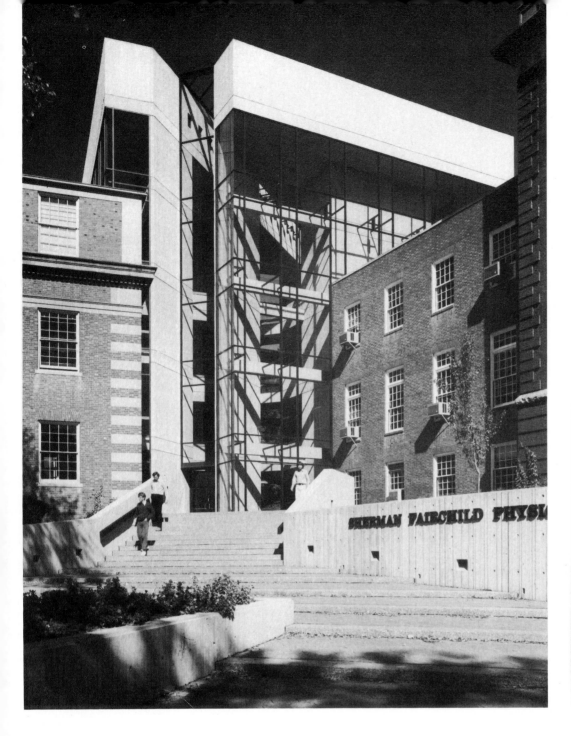

At the point at which the chemistry building and the physics building are linked by the tower, a broad entrance staircase has been created. The interconnecting floors can be seen through the glass facade. At night (below) the lighted tower becomes a landmark.

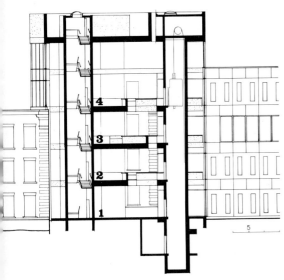

The end walls of the two older buildings have been left unaltered and are visible from the various levels within the tower. The poured concrete walls and piers are set back from the older walls, keeping them intact. As the photo (right) indicates, the old and new structural elements are attractively juxtaposed. Opening off the circulation elements are lounge spaces, called mini-commons, which provide opportunities for the students to rest and study.

RESIDENTIAL ADDITION

Here is an 80-year-old, rural house in Connecticut that has undergone minor cosmetic surgery several times in the past. None of these revisions, however, provided what was needed most: an adequate living room keyed to lawn spaces and to distant views. The existing living room was little more than an access way to the stairs and was virtually unfurnishable.

Mayers & Schiff strove to retain as much of the original character of the house as possible but to express the new addition for what it was. No attempt has been made to visually incorporate the new into the old or to erase the seam. The new living room is a double-height volume placed at 45 degrees to existing axes. It encloses at its upper level the existing eaves together with windows. Only the lower portion of the existing wall was removed and replaced with a structural column. In this manner, the old projects quite literally into the new, serving as a constant, vestigial reminder of what was, and making the new work an addition in the purest sense. To further emphasize the relationship between old and new, the existing horizontal siding was retained and contrasted to new finishes which are laid up diagonally.

The 45-degree offset of the addition opens direct views to the distant hills of the southeast and to large trees and lawn to the southwest—views that previously had been obliques.

There was, of course, a good deal of fun in the design to begin with. Mayers & Schiff retained much of it and added some of their own; but they were careful, in doing so, to solve real problems of comfort and function as well.

RESIDENTIAL ADDITION, Connecticut. Architects: *Mayers & Schiff*. Owners: *Martin and Lois Nadel.* Contractor: *Clifford Taber.*

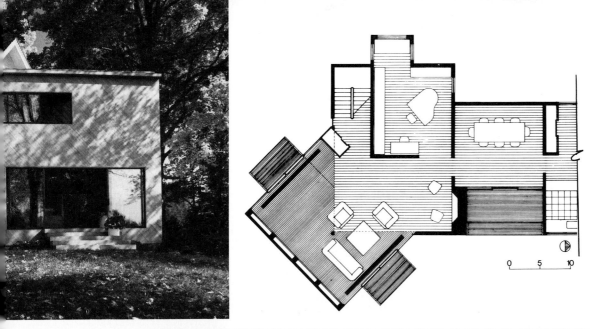

Bill Maris photos

THE EAST CAMBRIDGE SAVINGS BANK

In the view from the mezzanine above, the open quality between the new and old spaces can be fully appreciated—the new deriving visual richness by its proximity to the old and vice versa. The architects have purposely chosen to accentuate the differences in detailing and spatial concepts, so that there is no ambiguity between what was there and what has been added. By a successful contrast of scale, light, color and surfaces, the once dark original interior is enhanced. And new life has been brought to both a building and a downtown street.

In as facile and elegant a transition
from old to new as can be found anywhere,
architects Charles Hilgenhurst & Associates have
designed a light, airy and surprising addition to
an impeccably restored Massachusetts landmark—
surprising not just because of the ''fit,''
but because of the way that part of the older
building has been reused as if it were in a drawing
in exploded view

Similar to many older single-purpose buildings ranging from courthouses to stores, the East Cambridge Savings Bank is a familiar and distinctive landmark that might have been demolished because it was no longer adequate for the increasing complications and magnitude of its functions—even while arousing strong, possibly passionate sentiments in its owners, clients and passers-by. Fortunately, the irreplaceable qualities of such older buildings are being increasingly appreciated, and the decision—when function falters these days—may not be so much whether to tear down and start over as it is how to add on or alter without wrecking the imagery that was so valuable in the first place. Accordingly, the recent work of Charles Hilgenhurst & Associates in adapting this bank to new roles becomes an object lesson in adding on successfully. The elegant Byzantine

Revival landmark was optimistically built with the richest of materials—granite, marble, and bronze—at the height of the Great Depression in 1931. And its symmetrical form would have seemed to be complete in itself, so that no addition could be an improvement. But the architects have indeed enhanced the old building both by contrast in opening once-rather-somber interiors into bright new spaces and by carrying the current vogue for historical recall one step further. As can be seen in the photos above and right, the straightforward new construction is partially contained within a section of the older building's side facade that has been pushed forward to the street—a section that would have been covered by the new construction. And the wonderful composition that has resulted clearly enhances the visual importance of the whole bank, *and* the original part as well.

The new addition has been added to the right of the existing building in the photographs and in the isometric view above. By reusing a section of the granite facing from the side of the existing building as part of the addition, the architects have effectively extended the original street facade, while separating the two solid elements with a glazed connection that invites passers-by inside. And while creating a lively new image for the bank, the glazed connection has been designed to clearly state that the relocated facade is indeed an ''artifact.''

Commissioned to almost double by 9,000 square feet the size of the existing structure to accommodate staff offices and mortgage facilities, the architects not only met the requirements admirably, but provided a new, more accessible public image in that part of the addition that faces the street. By connecting the old facade and its relocated offspring with a recessed and lightly framed glass and plastic wall in such a way that the form of the older building keeps its three-dimensional character, the architects have also softened a once-formidable image by inviting the eyes of the passers-by into the new double height public reception area. To facilitate the relocation of the granite facing, the architects located the original quarry, which supplied the 50-year-old stonecutters' drawings. The new curved transparent wall is framed with steel mullions cut from half-inch-thick steel plate—with glass in wall sections, acrylic in the skylight. The structure is steel attached to the steel frame of the old building. The project has received an Award of Excellence from the American Institute of Steel Construction.

THE EAST CAMBRIDGE SAVINGS BANK, Cambridge, Massachusetts. Architects: *Charles G. Hilgenhurst & Associates—principal-in-charge: Charles Hilgenhurst; associate-in-charge: Robert Silver; design architects: Warren Schwartz, Robert Silver, William Buckingham; project manager: George Fisher; staff: Barbara Ford and William Powell.* Engineers: *Simpson, Gumpertz & Heger* (structural); BR + A (mechanical/electrical). General contractor: *Bond Brothers Incorporated.*

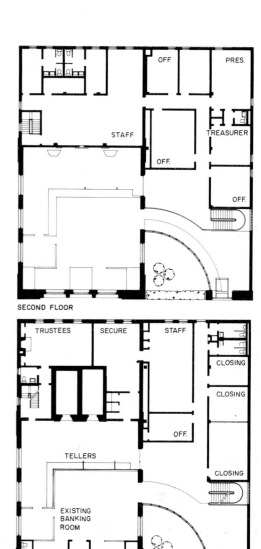

SECOND FLOOR

FLOOR

To accommodate functions that did not exist or were far less important when the original structure was built, the new addition provides a series of enclosed spaces behind a grand new reception area (photo left) that is an invitation to enter when passers-by look through the new curving glass wall. (Note the sympathetic way in which this wall meets the arched opening in what was the original outside wall.) The meticulously restored banking room is seen in the small photo at left.

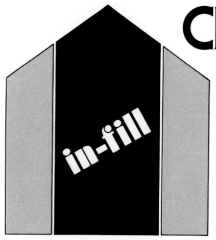

Chapter Four:

Adding onto buildings is logically followed by adding onto cities. Basically, the difference between inserting a new building into an existing urban setting, i.e., in-fill, and adding onto an individual building is one of scale. When designing an in-fill building, the architect must deal with a group of buildings and the spaces between them rather than with a specific building.

Yet, just as with smaller-scale contextual design problems, the concepts for an in-fill building range from reproducing the surroundings to sympathetically contrasting with them. Specifically, in-fill buildings may be designed as reproductions, abstractions, buildings based on urban design, background buildings, or buildings that become the focal point for their neighborhoods.

Examples of reproduction of existing buildings by well-known architects are rare. Yet, reproduction is a valid approach for an in-fill building when the existing group of buildings is strongly unified by a common architectural style. In such cases, the new building might not replicate any specific building, but would instead imitate a common style of the group. The danger of parody is, of course, ever present.

Rather than actually copying the stylistic language of the surrounding historic buildings, new buildings often attempt to capture the essence of their neighbors while remaining thoroughly contemporary. This can be done by picking up abstractions of the existing buildings, as discussed in the chapter on additions and as further illustrated in this chapter, or by responding to the larger-scaled factors of urban design. The spaces between buildings on streets and squares, views through these spaces, and the street pattern itself are some of the urban design factors upon which in-fill buildings may be based. By continuing or enhancing the basic organization of the existing urban setting, these new buildings become positive additions to the whole neighborhood.

Other buildings prefer to fit in by fading in. Rather than competing for the viewer's attention, some background buildings go unnoticed as an integral part of the total context. Some, such as the underground Nathan Pusey Library (p. 156), manage to almost disappear.

Antithetically, a new building may also be contextual in its conspicuousness. In the wrong place, this contrast is just one-upman-ship. But in an area of undistinguished buildings, the contrasting new building becomes the focal point for its environment. Rather than arrogantly intruding on the neighborhood, the in-fill actually gives an amorphous group of buildings their raison d'etre. Again, through sympathetic contrast, both old and new are enhanced.

Adding a new building to an existing group of buildings is a commonplace design problem. Yet our cities are proof that the compatible solution is uncommon. To strengthen the group, the new building must recognize and respond to the existing buildings. As with interiors, alterations, and additions, the response may range from continuing the existing character to contrasting with it. The following examples indicate the variety of forms possible within this range.

BEACON STREET APARTMENTS

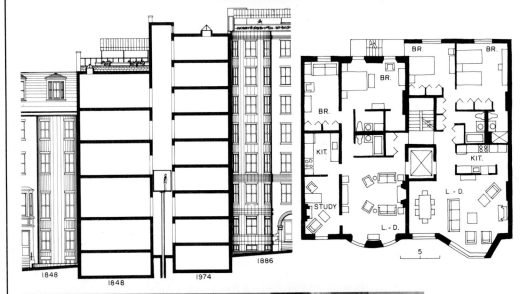

Fire destroyed one of a pair of Beacon Hill rowhouses in 1967, leaving a charred, gaping hole in the street facade until 1972 when architect James McNeely, in partnership with a local attorney, purchased the empty site and the undamaged bowfront next door.

The partners developed a plan to unite the two structures by serving both with a common elevator, stair and fire escape. Floor alignments could not be reconciled for the older structure had ceiling heights up to 14 feet. The new structure was designed with more standard eight foot ceilings (see section above). As a result, the elevator cab opens in both directions and stops within the shaft at different levels to serve either side.

In final form, the project includes 12 two bedroom apartments, two single-bedroom apartments and three studio apartments all sold as condominiums during construction or soon after. Those who purchased during construction had many choices in finish materials so the interiors vary considerably, reflecting a wide range of individual tastes. Common areas are kept to a minimum and maintenance charges, the architect reports, are among the lowest in Boston.

What is perhaps most important is that this well designed infill housing—the first of its kind in this Boston district—is housing of a type so many American cities desperately need. The new construction does not shoulder aside its older neighbors. It fits snugly into position respecting the scale, form and finish of adjoining buildings but keeps its own personality intact as it completes the street scene in a venerable but still handsome Boston neighborhood.

Architect: James McNeely
   16 Joy Street
   Boston, Massachusetts
Owners:
   Phoenix House Partners
Engineers:
   Craig Barnes (structural)
   Leo Brissette (mechanical)
Contractor: for building shell:
   John R. Clark & Associates
Photographer: William Owens

TRENTMAN RESIDENCE

Located amid the historic architecture of a quiet, tree-lined Georgetown street, this Washington, D.C. townhouse shows well that residential design can be contemporary and innovative, while respectful of an established neighborhood.

The architect's solution uses timeless materials in their natural state—burgundy-colored brick and gray slate—to keep the texture, scale and rhythm of the existing street. Materials combine with new interpretation of the traditional arch, bay window and mansard roof for a forceful design statement, in which the sculptured front bay windows especially are thoroughly modern in their expression of interior space.

Rooms were designed by the architect for a dramatic and uncluttered look usually found in a much larger house. Living room furnishings include silk and molded plastic or leather and chrome chairs. Floors are stained oak. Front rooms—the dining room and kitchen on the second floor and the master bedroom on the third—have a view of a park across the street. Back rooms—second-floor living room and other bedrooms —face a private garden. All are also oriented to two circular stair towers, which form the visual focal points of the house. Each stairwell includes view-through openings, and is capped with a 10-foot plastic dome to bring sunlight down through all the house. White walls and designed lighting add to the expansive quality of the scheme, which packs a great deal of comfort into an urban lot, thus offering its owners many qualities of a detached, suburban house with the many advantages of urban living.

The traditional townhouse, which fulfills a contemporary need, has, in this very spirited design, found a thoroughly contemporary expression.

RESIDENCE FOR MR. AND MRS. STEVEN TRENTMAN, Washington, D.C. Architect: *Hugh Newell Jacobsen.* Engineer: *James Madison Cutts.* Landscape architect: *Lester Collins.* Interiors: *Hugh Jacobsen.* Contractor: *The Brincefield Company.*

Behind their brick house, the owners can enjoy a secluded garden, equipped with fountain and slate floors on two levels and giving onto the living room via sliding aluminum doors. Kitchen and dining room are two steps up, a story above the entry. Special curved bricks were architect-designed.

Robert C. Lautman photos

INA TOWER

When an insurance outfit wants to make money with its money, one of the many things it can do is build what is called, in real estate parlance, an "investment-grade" structure. Which is what the 27-story INA Tower unabashedly is, hung by the fingernails to meet a tight budget on a tight, busy site. With these limitations or, more accurately, because of them, Mitchell/Giurgola has gotten up a street-smart building, as light in look as it is tight in means.

The skin of the building has all the tensile smoothness of a Lamborghini, and though it comes unnervingly close to looking like a machine-made object, there is more of the *process* of technology in this work than the finality of a finished, polished product. Kinetically, not statically, it is an integer factored out of its environment, signifying context.

Designed during a steel shortage, the base is of reinforced concrete, carrying bare steel shafts which rise to full metal framing above. The variegation of the curtain wall is not caprice, but climatic in nature, responding to the orientation of the facades and denoting the perimeter run of mechanicals. For example, on the upper portion of the south and west facades, as well as on the eastern face, the glass is recessed well behind the outer wall plane, this setback pointed up by curving soffits and sills. Naturally, this detail reduces heat and glare during summers. On the north facade, however, and on the lower portion of the southern one, which is shaded by a nearby building, the glass is flush, floor to ceiling. Where the recessed detail appears, those curved sills carry the induction units; elsewhere, the units stand freely.

The reality of the building's inhalation and exhalation is expressed mid-way up the tower, where the mechanical room is located. From here, the inductors are fed through shafts at the four corners. Air intakes on the north and south, exhausts on the east and west, show up like the flaring, cubistic nostrils that Picasso used to paint, and provide visual relief as juxtaposed with the tensility of the enamel-clad aluminum panels that compose the curtainwall below and above. The tower is as skillfully spliced into its environment as it is integral mechanically. Variations in lighting animate the pungent blues and golds of the lobby, which springs to a balcony level by way of a circular stair. And edging the streets, expansive shop windows of silicone-butted glass finish off any hint of separation between building and city. What a way for architecture to turn a significant corner.

INA TOWER, Philadelphia. Owner: *Insurance Company of North America.* Architects: *Mitchell/Giurgola Associates.* Engineers: *Skilling, Helle, Christiansen, Robertson* (structural); *Woodward-Gardner & Asso.* (foundations); *Joseph R. Loring & Associates* (mechanical/electrical). Consultants: *Howard Brandston* (lighting); *Robert A. Hansen* (acoustics). Contractor: *Brock-Keating Joint Venture.* (*Meridian Engineering, Inc., project manager*).

Rollin R. La France photos

A taut, tensile lightness characterizes the curtain walls of the INA Tower, an economical investment-grade structure which nevertheless brings off an almost luxurious sensibility of means and a marked attentiveness to the scale of the surrounding city. Recessed strips of window protect certain orientations from heat and glare; flush glass opens up the interior from the north (opposite).

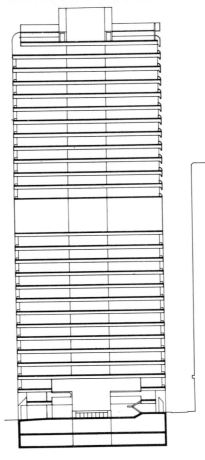

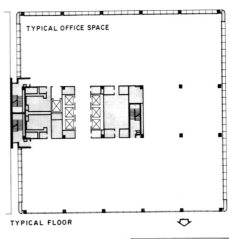

TYPICAL OFFICE SPACE

TYPICAL FLOOR

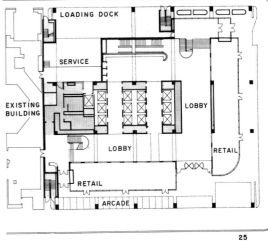

LOADING DOCK

SERVICE

EXISTING BUILDING

LOBBY

LOBBY

RETAIL

RETAIL

ARCADE

STREET LEVEL

25

No monument in terms of cost, the INA Tower is monumentally compelling as a work of both technological skill and environmental design. Fully sprinklered inside, with equipment for early smoke detection, its alternate facade treatments, modulating the admission of sunlight in accord with orientation, helps keep operating costs low due to minimized energy waste, according to the client. In line with stringent budget, the columnless interiors are spare. But in the more public spaces, like the blue and gold lobby (above, below), the simplicity is elegant due to the careful handling of lighting, the practical gesture of the circular stair, and the intriguing juxtaposition of the first floor and balcony levels, where the K-braced structural bents cut diagonally through at the perimeter of the core.

At streetside, the INA Tower is spliced into the life and movement of the city. Two levels of shops open the building to passersby, while contrasting facade treatment at the base, enlivened by the play of recessed bays, create an interesting structural texture as the building turns the corner (top left). Contrasts between the tight, tensile, smooth-finished facades and adjacent buildings are denoted with carefully designed, considerate details (bottom left). Together, old and new become a mutually sympathetic mapping of the on-going, built-up spontaneous nature of the city.

WESTLAKE MALL

Site: Portions of two downtown city blocks (between 4th and 5th Avenues and Olive and Pine Streets) presently in active use (not cleared)

Project: Westlake Mall

Mix: Public and private funds, public and private use. Functional types: urban park, retail mall, hotel, monorail terminal, parking garage, multiple movie theaters, public plaza designed as sculpture garden. Future: residential development adjacent

Links: Relocated monorail terminus and terminal, elevated pedestrian plaza connecting to adjacent Times Square Building, and "retail bridges" connecting to three department stores on the other sides of the site.

Spin-off: Possible recycling of adjacent Times Square Building as new extension of Seattle Art Museum, and possible residential development in the "Denny Regrade" area to the north of the Westlake project.

Developer: Mondev International, Ltd.

Architects: Mitchell/Giurgola Architects—team: Romaldo Giurgola, Jan Keane (project architect), George Yu, Sigrid Miller, Ted Chapin, Randy Leach. Consultants—Skilling Helle Christiansen and Robertson, structural engineering (Leslie Robertson, partner-in-charge); Joseph R. Loring Associates, mechanical engineering.

Associated architect: Joyce Copeland Vaughan and Nordfors Architects (Lee Copeland, partner-in-charge).

Community: Department of Community Development

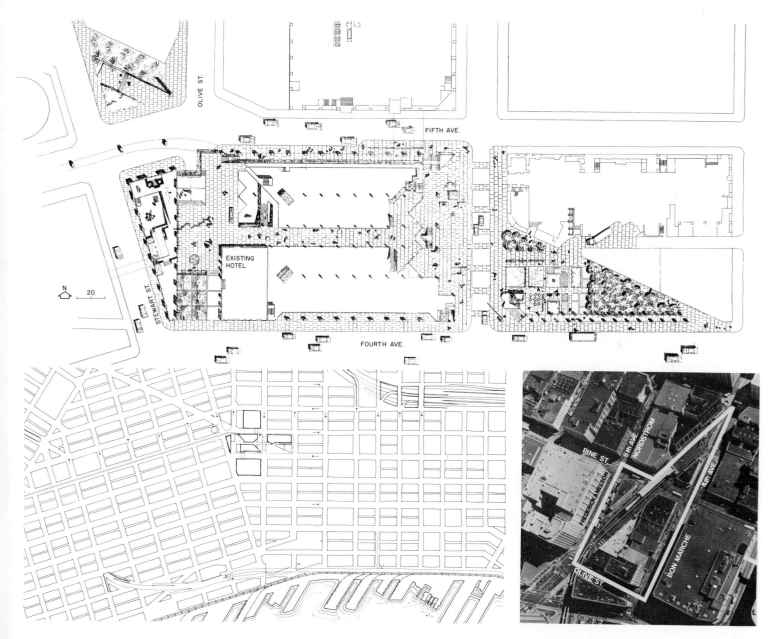

Romaldo Giurgola says: "Mondev came to our office with a program that was only in its formative stages, embryonic. It was an idea about the center of a city. And the problem here is quite a different one from Colorado Springs, for example. Here there are not open ground and abandoned parking areas, but a very vital section of the city—people, shops and three large department stores. So it was dealing with material that is already alive and in place, which means the whole process will be quite different, because it will imply a constant relocation and provision for the people who are actually presently working on the site, so that the development will take place with full recognition that the life will go on exactly as it is now, and probably with some new potential developing within it."

Seattle's project is not urban renewal, and the situation Giurgola describes is, in fact, the reverse of the familiar sequence in urban renewal—first acquisition and demolition, then planning, then implementation, all as separate steps in what has tended to be a very long process indeed. Ransen and Bacon are convinced that this separation of planning from implementation in the renewal process has been a critical barrier to effective participation by developers in it. (Bacon says there is "an absolutely tragical lack of understanding of the positive role of the developer. The whole role of the developer has got to be re-thought and reconsidered.")

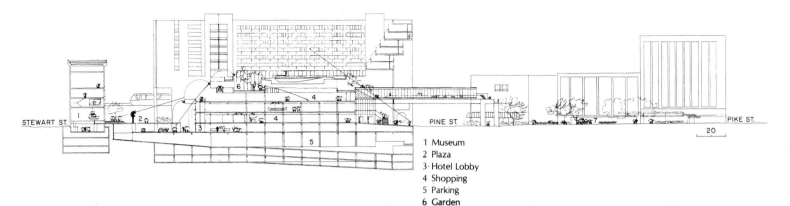

1 Museum
2 Plaza
3 Hotel Lobby
4 Shopping
5 Parking
6 Garden
7 Park

The site is at the juncture of two of Seattle's multiple grids, just south of the old Times Square Building whose triangular shape marks the juncture. The change in grid and the city's development pattern have effectively divided the city in two for many years. Westlake Mall will reunite it by linking the main business section to the south with the Times Square Building if, as suggested, it becomes an extension of the Seattle Art Museum. The Mondev proposal would relocate the monorail terminus to one side of the site, parallel to Fifth Avenue, and close Olive Way (the street between the site and the Times Square Building) to create a pedestrian plaza connection between the Mall and the Times Square Building.

The proposed new building would share its site with the existing Mayflower Hotel (rectangular building at right in model photo), the only building on the site scheduled to be retained. The design concept puts an eight-story hotel above three levels of retailing and an underground parking garage. "Retail bridges" would make pedestrian connections to the department stores on three sides of the site, and an elevated pedestrian plaza would connect with the Times Square Building on the fourth side. The opposite end of the new building would open on a 25,000-square-foot triangular park. Hotel rooms would overlook a landscaped interior court, which would be open at both ends.

Rollin R. La France

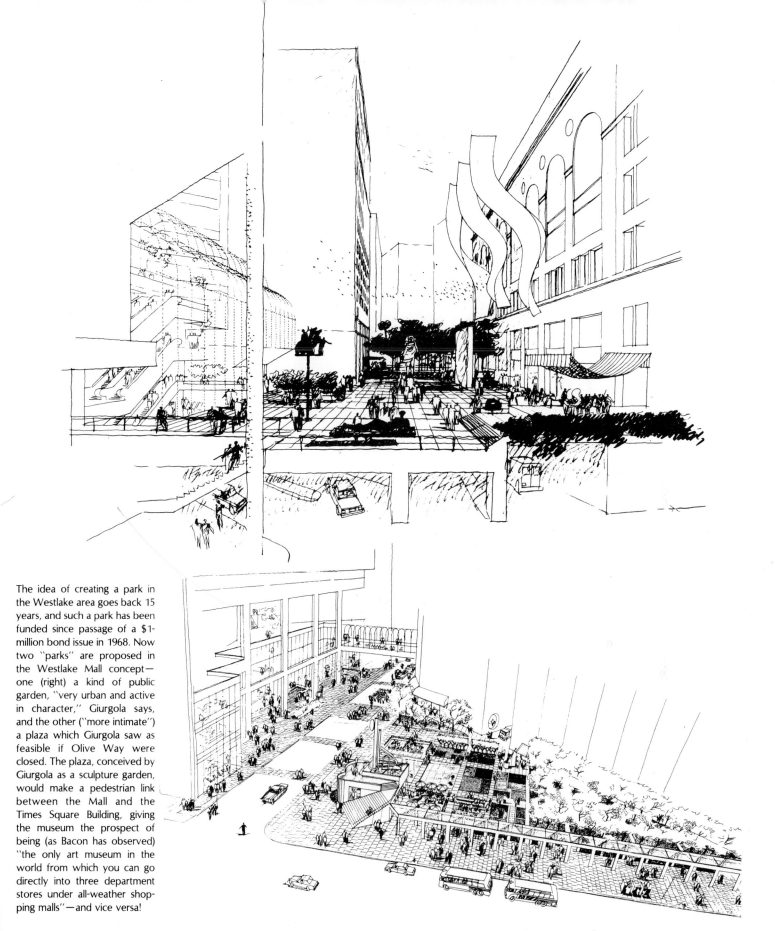

The idea of creating a park in the Westlake area goes back 15 years, and such a park has been funded since passage of a $1-million bond issue in 1968. Now two "parks" are proposed in the Westlake Mall concept— one (right) a kind of public garden, "very urban and active in character," Giurgola says, and the other ("more intimate") a plaza which Giurgola saw as feasible if Olive Way were closed. The plaza, conceived by Giurgola as a sculpture garden, would make a pedestrian link between the Mall and the Times Square Building, giving the museum the prospect of being (as Bacon has observed) "the only art museum in the world from which you can go directly into three department stores under all-weather shopping malls"—and vice versa!

In Seattle, selection of the developer came first, not last; and funds that in many cities would have been paid to consultants for a "development plan" on which developers would *later* be invited to bid were therefore available to Mondev to hire its own consultant (i.e., Giurgola) and develop its own proposal out of the kind of intensive interchange among developer, architect and community described in the article on the concept planning process.

In Seattle, a mayor strongly committed to the project had a strongly professional Community Planning Department to speak for the community in that developer-architect-community planning process.

So the "development plan" for Westlake Mall had its implementation plan built into it through the participation in the planning process of a developer ready to commit $50-million to the execution of that very $60-million plan.

In what may be a unique procedure in a project of this scale, the city of Seattle is acquiring the site by negotiation. And in another unusual effort, tenants now on the site will be temporarily relocated during demolition and construction phases, then moved into quarters in the new building.

Giurgola says: "Mondev came into the office with a will to build, and that was the refreshing thing."

EAST BUILDING OF THE NATIONAL GALLERY OF ART

In May of 1969, Ieoh Ming Pei, kept company by a couple of his designers, sat patiently on one of the stone benches outside of the board room of the National Gallery of Art in Washington.

After something of a wait, Paul Mellon, the president of the Gallery, came out into the hall, followed by J. Carter Brown and John Walker. Mr. Brown, who was in the process of taking over as director of the Gallery from Mr. Walker, his boss, mentor, and friend of eight years, had a big boyish grin on his face.

Mr. Mellon, who is understated, said they had decided. After two years of thinking about how the National Gallery of Art should grow, and after six solid months of Mr. Pei's having absorbed himself and his sharpest "pencils" in coming up with a concept for its projected East Building, the scheme was in, most satisfactory, and so let's go.

Mr. Pei did. Right over to the house of his friend Joseph Alsop, the columnist, who broke out some bottles of champagne, *Dom Perignon* champagne, while Mr. Pei, using some yellow blue-lined legal paper, explained (still exploring, no doubt) the nature of his concept. What they sipped, and what he sketched, were vintage.

Nine years later, on the first of June, the East Building—containing galleries around a glowing courtyard, a Center for Advanced Study in the Visual Arts, and an underground concourse connecting it with the Gallery's neoclassical original by John Russell Pope—was opened by President Jimmy Carter.

Though it is not popularly understood that he likes architecture almost as much as music and poetry, the President's interest was not lost on those who were crowded onto the new plaza, which is covered with four-inch cubic cobblestones of Oklahoma granite, and which is 375 feet wide.

In one of the most illuminating references to architecture made recently by an American leader, Mr. Carter not only "critiqued" the East Building as a study in urban compatibility and considerate proportion, but he also went further, explaining how it symbolizes the increasingly supportive connection between public life and art.

It might be said that the most expressive, useful art is doing everything well. The seat of American government, as laid out by Major Pierre L'Enfant in the late 18th Century, was started up in that spirit. The East Building—paid for by Paul Mellon, Alisa Mellon Bruce (his late sister), and the Andrew W. Mellon Foundation (Andrew W. Mellon, their father, paid for the original, which opened in 1941)—now consolidates that spirit.

This intent as interpreted by Mr. Pei runs deeper than munificence, the costs having come to over $94 million—for creative conviction is summoned by other factors, and more valuable ones; such manifest, mesmeric beauty is not merely purchased.

The lessons of the East Building are in the intensity, competence, and passion that were spent in the designing of it, and, as seen to by the Chas. H. Tomkins Co., the builder, in the doing of it. Besides Mr. Brown looking after the Gallery's concerns (he grew up in a house by Richard Neutra, complete with two of Buckminster Fuller's Dymaxion bathrooms), there were David Scott, seeing to the programming of space, and Hurley Offenbacher, seeing to construction.

Excellence sometimes exacts terrific tribute of this kind—but it rewards those who

The second major section of the East Building is the Center for Advanced Study in the Visual Art, its six stories rising around a reading-and-reference hall that recalls, without literally rendering, a medieval library (page 118, above). Its entrance, like those of the adjacent exhibition area, is low, compressive, and anticipatory (page 118, bottom), releasing movement and vistas that are illuminated by light coming in from the southeast and southwest, but still defined by the enfolding presence of the concrete edges of floor dramatically dovetailed with the bounding walls of marble. This space, 70 feet high, is also edged with book stacks and scholars' offices, which, rather than stuck off somewhere, fully share in (fulfilling really) the light and loftiness of the hall. The uppermost level of the Center is taken up by administrative offices, a board room and a refectory that are interconnected by a passage running past an outdoor terrace and a skylit stairwell (right). Variations of the triangle permeate the place from the configuration of the skylights to the deeply recessed coffers of the ceiling down in the concourse-level auditorium.

dig down deep to pay it with an assuredness and serenity that finally belie the pains, perplexities, and bruises along the road. That kind of tribute was paid here, and a lot of money—as the program and the budget, though both were strictly monitored, blossomed beyond an earlier concept for a study center with ~~~ ~~~

This ~~~
between Penns, ~~~
though—a trapezoidal ~~~
acres, that had been set aside ~, ~~~~~ ~~
the late 1930s when it accepted Andrew W. Mellon's gift. Was just a study center, a more or less private enclave, really right at such a strategic, symbolic point—especially so when the National Gallery of Art had been envisioned as quite a public affair?

A sense of accountability came into play, something that the Mellons have never ignored, even though it meant that an early estimate of $20 million was not going to be enough to make the East Building the public affair that their civic and cultural consciousness was impelling. Paul Mellon had the vision not to panic, and fortunately the means. He ended up giving the kind of gift that he would have liked to receive.

The lessons of the East Building are also in how this complicated cycle of programmatic and budgetary decisions, of planning options and horrific staging problems, were brought into alignment and given a cohesion that is indeed assured and serene. Its complexity is all the more awesome because it is agreeably concealed.

Then there are lessons in how the design was developed, not as an object, but as a latticework of objectives. Its material configuration of marble, concrete, and glass derives from, deferring to, the physical, spatial, and symbolic elements of the city. The ceremonious diagonal of Pennsylvania Avenue edges the site on the north. The Mall edges it on the south. Fourth Street edges the site on the west, with Mr. Pope's immaculate monumentality beyond, and Third Street edges it on the east. It is a flying wedge of axial forces aimed at the Capitol, where money is appropriated for the Gallery's operations.

Mr. Pei's aim was to take these forces into account. There were setback lines to respect, too, as established by the National Capitol Planning Commission; and height restrictions relative to Pennsylvania Avenue and the Mall (at substantially different cornice levels), as established by the Commission of Fine Arts. Then there was Mr. Pope's proposition—its deft gradations of Tennessee marble, its central rotunda and flanking sculpture halls, the height of its moat-like walls extending out to and edging Constitution Avenue just before it converges with Pennsylvania, its strong east-west axis and the symmetry of its east-facing facade. All posed crucial questions for contemporary judgment. Mr. Pei's team was listening hard, looking for contextual clues, and gratefully picked up on those of Major L'Enfant and Mr. Pope.

Those listening and looking have included Leonard Jacobson, the project architect, Thomas Schmitt, the project designer,

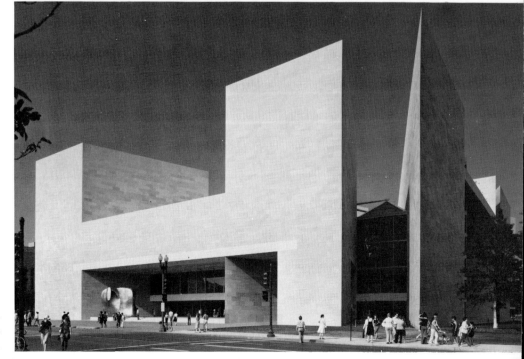

The East Building of the National Gallery of Art infers the geometry of its trapezoidal site, adjusting itself to the scale of Pennsylvania Avenue (below right) and of the Mall (below left). This geometry is articulated by the interlocking and interplay of two basic triangles—an isoceles section containing the exhibition areas, and a right triangle containing the Center for Advanced Study in the Visual Arts. The isoceles section is entered from Fourth Street, passing a burnished bronze by Henry Moore, symmetrically aligned across a new plaza from the original Gallery building (left). Also in from Fourth is the entrance to the Center, through a deep indentation which not only introduces the section composed of the right triangle but also a subtle but definite shift to asymmetry in the direction of the Mall (opposite below). The grammar of marble and concrete (above) is clearly, cleanly enunciated.

and William Jakabek, the job captain. Also, and with lasting value, designers Yann Weymouth and William Pederson, beginning in 1968, had worked closely with Mr. Pei on the initially submitted scheme, and Mr. Weymouth had been asked for some procedural advice by John Walker, early in 1967, when the Gallery was first trying to figure out how to solve some grievous spatial limitations of the old building and get the grounds ready for some new growing room. (Mr. Weymouth and Mr. Pederson struck out on their own early in 1971.)

In September of 1969, beginning a severe four-month-long charette to refine the scheme in the context of also defining a set of programmatic and budgetary options about how much to build and how much to defer, Leonard Jacobson assumed day-to-day control. On into 1970, Thomas Schmitt began shouldering the design challenges. *There were some.* Getting into 1971, a major (and fortunate) shift occurred. This was in the courtyard, which had been largely layered over with a heavy coffered slab, and its skylight design, which had an incongruous array of egg-shell-style lights up there. The surfaces, space, light and, most crucially, the art did not appear that they would be right enough together as embodied in that first scheme. The architects began an even more intensive attack on the design. Though the basic plan did not change, the present lyricism and luminosity of circulation from level to level was achieved. For the first time, too, an entry directly into the Study Center from the courtyard was arranged for.

Earlier on, the plot thickening, that trapezoid had been transformed into two interlocking triangles, a kind of Romeo-and-Juliet geometry. One triangle (for exhibitions) isosceles, measuring 405 by 405 by 270; the second (for the Center for Advanced Study in the Visual Arts), a right triangle, measuring 405 by 135 by 381.

Come out here on the Fourth Street side. Mr. Pei explains, ``I am quite pleased with the way one gets into the building. You see, we had to have a way to get into the gallery area, and a second way to get into the study center area—and we were permitted entry only from Fourth. The Mall side was closed to us for this purpose, and Pennsylvania Avenue too. This was the most difficult problem we faced, making two entrances on this same side—one very public, the other comparatively private. Now there is no doubt, coming up here, about which is which, and Henry Moore's bronze, which is titled *Knife Edge Mirror Two Piece,* certainly enhances the public experience of getting inside. This problem relates to another—recognizing and reconciling the symmetry of the older building. So the isosceles section of the new building is symmetrically aligned with the old one; *it has to be.* By making this deep indentation for the entrance to the study center, there is a necessary (and quite natural) shift toward asymmetry—and to the scale of the Mall in contrast to that of the Avenue. The spandrel up there continues the cornice line of the buildings along the Mall, in fact. Facing

Space, light, and movement—now spontaneous, now processional—are the reality of the courtyard rising 80 feet above the concourse-level entrance to the exhibition areas (above). Looking up into, or across, the courtyard, the four-foot-thick floor levels and post-tensioned bridges overlap and interconnect at various points as people thread in and out of the four gallery levels. Grand stairs from the concourse, and a second sweep up to the mezzanine (below) give way to a run of escalators leading to the third, major level with a terrace cafe, the second bridge sweeping across the northeastern area of the upper courtyard (opposite, below left), and the larger ranges of gallery space. Light dapples down.

these problems as *one problem* called for balancing symmetry and asymmetry.''

The angle of Pennsylvania Avenue to the east-west axis of the Gallery literally engendered the basic geometry and, within it, the basic module. That angle, a touch under 20 degrees, was found to account for a miniscule four-inch discrepancy when calculated along the Pennsylvania Avenue elevation, a touch over 450 feet long. The triangular module was thus set—pervading this place, *being* this place. By taking the two long legs out 20 degrees each way, for a total of 40 degrees, the other two angles of this module being generated become 70 degrees each. These long legs of the module measure 15 feet, because 15 goes into 450 feet evenly; and the short leg of the module is 10.

In many respects this building is for all seasons and architects—a countenance of precedent which, in principle, has been working for quite some time. It is also a calm commentary about the commotion, inquiry, and cant that have been heard, these same nine years, about the supposedly limited language of modern architecture. It could not be less modern, actually, or more modern. It could not be less postmodern, as it were, or more. What is ''modern,'' anyway? As Frank Lloyd Wright used to say, ''Come on, fellows, let's not concern ourselves with these matters of *taste*.''

The East Building has an identity, integrity, and drama of its own. People (by the thousands, every day now) walk or wing on vectors of experience, perception, encounter—up into, across, around the homing device of the 70-foot-high courtyard with its 20-foot-high ficus trees, circular benches, and works of art. It is covered by a triangular cluster of 25 tetrahedronal skylights, which takes up 16,000 square feet, measuring 225 feet on the long sides and 150 on the shorter one. It is a clearing in the forest of the city, the precedent of Mr. Pope's rotunda, come again, at once encased and enlivened by the compressive presence of newly quarried Tennessee marble, and by the tensional runs of concrete beams, soffits, four-foot-thick floor slabs, bridges spanning the space as physical and symbolic sources of connection, and the triangularly coffered ceilings.

This marble has been laid up in the same two-by-five-foot pieces that were used by Mr. Pope, and with the same one-eighth-of-an-inch joints. The pieces were selected from the same quarries in Knoxville by Malcolm Rice, who worked on the original.

Yet this new one is not a marble building in the sense of its being marble through and through. Three-inch-thick cladding was the means, the metaphor, of relating to Mr. Pope's material, which Mr. Mellon felt was important. The older building really *was* marble, over a foot thick, and in such an ecstasy of compression that the joints are practically indiscernible, waterproof, and maintenance-free. So are Mr. Pei's joints, though. Each piece is ingeniously floated, independently, and the joints are filled with a lining of neoprene—no cracks, no caulking. These marble surfaces, some of them

116

Entering the exhibition area either from the plaza on Fourth Street or by a low tunnel leading to it from the cafeteria below the plaza (opposite below), the upper galleries are unfolded within three ''houses'' or ''pods,'' one rising up from each of the three corners of the isosceles triangle encasing this section. Each ''house'' is a parallelogram, with elevators or spiral stairs set into the corners (below left), and the healthy room-like scale of the galleries is thus arranged, with great flexibility of expression and installation, within basic hexagonal hollows within these ''houses.'' Walls are freshly built to suit the scale or spirit of the art being shown, both enclosure and culture looking permanently at home (opposite above); the uppermost ceilings in each ''house'' are freshly adjusted, up or down, assuring apt vertical scale, as in this installation of David Smith's *Voltri* series (below right).

hundreds of feet long, and without expansion joints, do serve precedent. But technically, Mr. Pei, for whom marble was not a familiar (or particularly favorite) material, set precedent in patentable terms. Mr. Rice also saw to it that the pieces were selected in such a way—the marble has gradations of brown shading into pink—that the subtleties of the original building have been simulated.

It is very useful to look at what Mr. Pope and Mr. Rice did together, way back when. The darker gradations, starting at the base, work around and up into the lighter gradations, the lightest marble of all being in the dome over the rotunda. And look at the eight columns on the north or south portico. The outermost columns are of darker gradation, becoming gradually lighter, from either direction, toward the center.

This is the kind of care that Mr. Pei has successfully interpreted on his own turf and terms, though due to unexpected shortages of certain gradations and unpredictable delivery schedules, the light-to-dark gradations on the outside of the East Building are more abrupt in some places than they were intended to be. Weathering will eventually fulfill that intention.

The architectural concrete is beyond doubt fulfilled. It is the equivalent of precious stone. During design, the relationship of its color and texture to the marble was seriously pondered. Should they be closely compatible or contrasting? Concrete signified more than structural capacity and, with a lot of steel embedded in it, great spans; it was the means, and the metaphor, of relating to our own century. So maintaining contrast, relative to the marble, seemed consistent.

The concrete was poured into formwork of fir which was nothing less than *brilliant* cabinetry, and the faintest tint of the pinkish powdered marble was mixed into it. The resulting color of the concrete, resembling the light of dawn, resonates throughout the building, discreetly but definitely maintaining contact with the lighter, rarer gradations of the marble. Mr. Pope over there had used the lightest, rarest marble for his dome—a kind of marble no longer available. Mr. Pei, over here, with this concrete, has achieved that kind of subtlety—a hue that becomes the harmonics of his composition.

Inside the clearing—that courtyard—the third basic material of the East Building, natural light, comes down through the facets of the tetrahedrons, which are fitted with sunscreens. Their delicate rounded members filter the light, deflecting and diffusing it, dappling the bounding walls, especially the vast northern wall above the court, with effects worthy of the Expressionist masters—or of Louis Kahn.

The amazing feat in all of this is that what is commonly thought of as "material" (the marble, the concrete) has been dematerialized; what is commonly thought of as intangible, weightless, and even metaphysical (this light in here) has been *materialized*. More than a confluence of surfaces, triangularly configured, this wonderful room is a confluence of forces, wafting in and out with an

118

order that Kepler would have found comfort-able, and which is also being found to be companionable by people not inclined to dwell on "cosmic harmonies." It is not too much to say that inside this big isosceles triangle is one of the most resplendent rooms of all time. Perhaps Mr. Pei, in the manner of Mr. Kahn, asked precedent what it wanted to be and it said, "This."

The design in all of its dimensions is also a successful *working* museum. J. Carter Brown, as it turned out, was every bit as much the architect in this regard. There is something about museums, a good many of them anyway, that Mr. Brown was determined to avoid. Too many are intimidating; too many are fatiguing. There is often a feeling of wanting to get out somehow, or of being lost, or of missing something.

Those museums done in fealty to infinite flexibility often leave people wondering whether they have come to look at exhibitions or to look at staff and workmen changing exhibitions. And then there is the museum-as-shrine, pristinely poised on classi-cized plinths. A few great paintings and sculptures, placed sensitively about heady vast-nesses to resemble one of Mies van der Rohe's collages, do not necessarily inspire mere mortals to incarcerate themselves, as they must in Mies' magic box in Berlin, down-stairs in the plinth where most of the art is kept. This is a case of art shooting itself through a temple, and Mr. Brown, who undertook a serious study of museums all over America and Europe with the architects, was not about to be caught holding a smok-ing gun of a building. Neither, of course, was Mr. Pei, who, though admiring Mies as much as any thoughtful student of culture must, readily warmed to Mr. Brown's concept of the museum-as-*house*.

This means, among other things, a feel-ing of family, a recurring, confiding familiarity, and of rooms—a healthy domestic scale, more simply. Mr. Brown wanted houses—which is what the three towers rising from the corners of the isosceles triangle have come to be called, although some working on the job came to call them "pods."

He also wanted a sense of centrality and orientation—a *place* where one can be "born" into the building and, from any level, from any range of rooms, where one can readily be "born" again. This place is the courtyard, and entering it from Fourth Street, moving beneath the coffers of the 10-foot-high ceiling there, one is released into the space and light—and more.

On the outside, from all around, the towers could be seen rising up, anchoring the corners of the building. The filigree of the skylight—a space frame of steel members pitching up and joined together with nodes of cast steel—could be seen triangulating itself between the towers like a composite of crystals embedded high on the ledge of a canyon. Yet inside, which seems outside, these anchoring houses assume another, if recollective, position. Looking up through the skylight, they can be seen rising up again. They do not loom though; the members of

The cladding of Tennessee marble is detailed, even at the most acute exterior corners, to maintain a quality of solidness, cutting the pieces to avoid joints at the corners themselves and avoiding any veneer-like effects. The vertical section and cut-away view at the bottom of the page illustrate how the two-by-five-foot pieces are individually attached to pre-cast blocks in the backing wall. Steel plates support the bottom corners; anchors restrain the tops; neoprene lining accepts expansion.

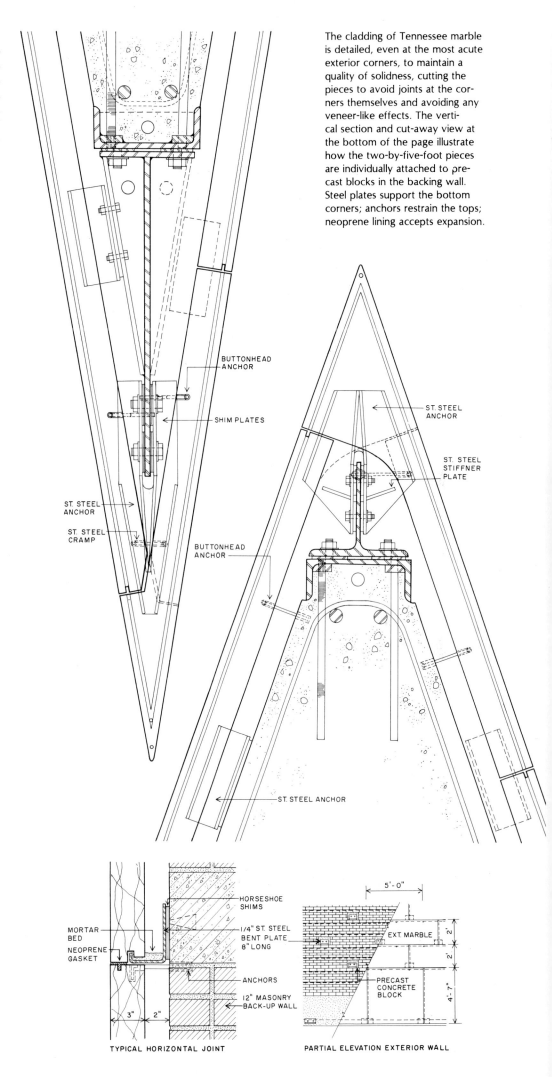

BUTTONHEAD ANCHOR

SHIM PLATES

ST. STEEL ANCHOR

ST. STEEL CRAMP

BUTTONHEAD ANCHOR

ST. STEEL ANCHOR

ST. STEEL ANCHOR

ST. STEEL STIFFNER PLATE

MORTAR BED

NEOPRENE GASKET

HORSESHOE SHIMS

1/4" ST. STEEL BENT PLATE 8" LONG

ANCHORS

12" MASONRY BACK-UP WALL

TYPICAL HORIZONTAL JOINT

EXT. MARBLE

PRECAST CONCRETE BLOCK

5'- 0"

PARTIAL ELEVATION EXTERIOR WALL

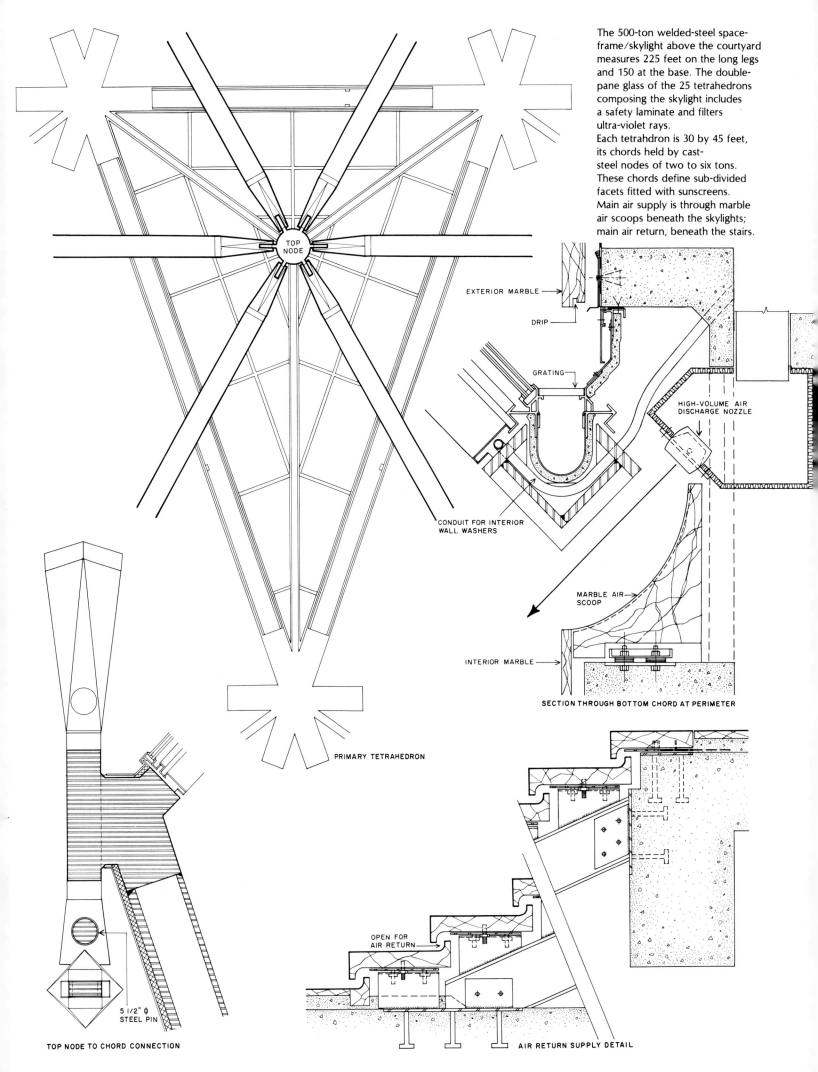

The 500-ton welded-steel space-frame/skylight above the courtyard measures 225 feet on the long legs and 150 at the base. The double-pane glass of the 25 tetrahedrons composing the skylight includes a safety laminate and filters ultra-violet rays.

Each tetrahdron is 30 by 45 feet, its chords held by cast-steel nodes of two to six tons. These chords define sub-divided facets fitted with sunscreens. Main air supply is through marble air scoops beneath the skylights; main air return, beneath the stairs.

TOP NODE

EXTERIOR MARBLE

DRIP

GRATING

HIGH-VOLUME AIR DISCHARGE NOZZLE

CONDUIT FOR INTERIOR WALL WASHERS

MARBLE AIR SCOOP

INTERIOR MARBLE

SECTION THROUGH BOTTOM CHORD AT PERIMETER

PRIMARY TETRAHEDRON

5 1/2" ⌀ STEEL PIN

TOP NODE TO CHORD CONNECTION

OPEN FOR AIR RETURN

AIR RETURN SUPPLY DETAIL

the sunscreens, giving the light its almost material diversity of shapes and sensations, also renders them like *memories*, memories of something experienced more tangibly earlier, rather than as solid sentinels.

As much as the geometrical theme delivers unity here, (the triangle-as-diety stops just short of having influenced the shape of the doorknobs), there is repeated surprise: images and vistas overlapping, variations played and picked up on again from level to level, like a fugue. Math and music are sublimated in each other and wisely unfrozen. (Mr. Pei's and Mr Schmitt's decision, back there in 1971, to lighten up the sense of overhead load and soften the hard surfaces with a more effervescent circulation system was extremely smart, courageous, and really makes the building.) The houses, up there now, with many different kinds of exhibitions in (as one gradually learns) many shapes and sensations of format, raise anticipation, like refreshing breezes coming up.

This is as dramatically evident coming into from the lower concourse of the East Building, which stretches over here beneath the plaza, connecting to the old building, where a new lobby has been laboriously but neatly chipped out, by way of a cafeteria.

This concourse is effectively a separate building, passing under Fourth Street. Doing it solved a maze of costly problems related to having to build under Fourth, and keep the assorted services and utilities running there while keeping the street open to traffic.

The concourse splices into the East Building by way of a low, long tunnel with a long, slow-moving sidewalk. This instrument focuses anticipation as it *v-e-e-r-y* gradually takes one eastward from the cafeteria area toward the concourse level of the courtyard space where a blue-and-yellow tapestry by Jean Arp beckons. This movement is along a skewed axis, deflected from the main east-west axis of the old building, and parallel to that of Pennsylvania Avenue in alignment with the geometry of the new building. The effect of walking off the moving sidewalk, out into the light coming way down into this concourse level, is dramatically swept up marble stairs to the main floor, with the wide bridge of the mezzanine level (reached by a second sweep) hovering above. These stairs quite grandly recall a processional event, a quality of occasion, like fanfares.

Another allusion to history hangs above, from the skylight. A black-and-red mobile by Alexander Calder, with arms stretching out as much as 70 feet, sprinkles the space with lightweight aluminum petals as the whole thing, Mr. Calder's last work, weighing only 700 pounds, glides around the room. In its slow, even, circular excursion it defines a zone recalling the dome of Mr. Pope's rotunda. This mobile, engineered by Paul Matisse, a relative of Henri Matisse, is kept moving, humorously enough, by redirecting the building's air supply system, which works through curved reveals running along the upper edge of the bounding marble walls. When the mobile was first hung up, it would not get moving. Engineers fretted, along with every-

BASEMENT
1. Bookstacks
2. Mechanical
3. Staff parking
4. Service
5. Green room
6. Toilets
7. Auditorium

CONCOURSE LEVEL
1. Photo archives
2. Books receiving
3. Slides
4. Photo lab
5. Data processing
6. Special exhibitions
7. Auditorium
8. Lounge
9. Moving walkway
10. Mechanical
11. Workshops
12. Service corridor
13. Offices
14. Art storage
15. Chadar
16. Cafe
17. Dining
18. Restaurant
19. Kitchen
20. Sales
21. Truck dock
22. Lobby

GROUND LEVEL 1
1. Reading
2. Call desk
3. Reading room
4. Periodicals-catalogs
5. Gallery
6. Sculpture pool
7. Information
8. Orientation
9. Exhibit
10. Study center entrance
11. Coats
12. Gallery entrance
13. Sculpture
14. Fountain
15. Chadar
16. Skylights

MEZZANINE LEVEL 2
1. Library offices
2. Stacks
3. NGA Press
4. Gallery
5. Sculpture
6. Sales Desk
7. Office
8. Toilets

LEVEL 3
1. Study offices
2. Stacks
3. Print storage
4. Print reading

MAIN GALLERY LEVEL 4
1. Offices
2. Stacks
3. Lounge
4. Gallery
5. Terrace cafe
6. Kitchen

LEVEL 5
1. Curatorial offices
2. Stacks
3. Education staff
4. Gallery

LEVEL 6
1. Curatorial offices
2. Administration offices

LEVEL 7
1. Assistant director
2. Director
3. President
4. Board room
5. Terrace
6. Offices
7. Roof garden
8. Refectory
9. Kitchen

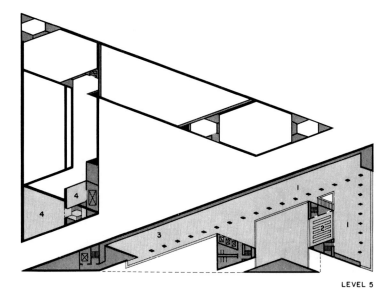

LEVEL 5

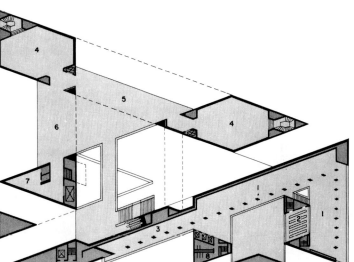

LEVEL 2   MEZZANINE

Entrance to the East Building is through the concourse level, coming over from a new lobby that has been laboriously but skillfully carved out of the original Gallery's east entrance, and through a large cafeteria. Or entrance is through the ground-level area in from Fourth Street and a new plaza with tetrahedral skylights into the cafeteria and a range of fountains. This low ground-level entrance introduces the skylit courtyard, and the three towers (one at each of the three corners of the courtyard) housing galleries. Grand stairs rise from the concourse and courtyard; the mezzanine with its bridge loading to exhibitions or, up an escalator and across a second bridge, to the main gallery level of 20,000 square feet. The topmost gallery is tidily housed on the fifth level. Recurrent visual and physical reference is made to the unifying courtyard throughout; museum fatigue has been routed.

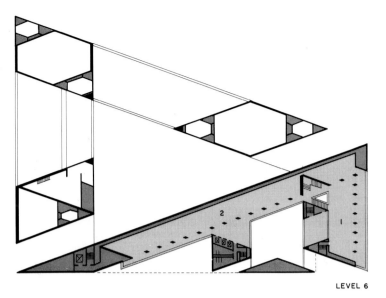

LEVEL 6

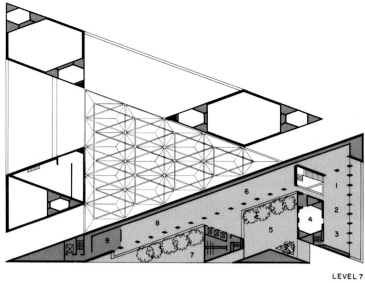

LEVEL 7

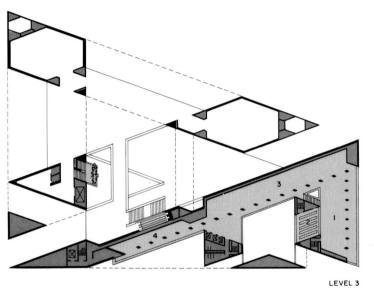

LEVEL 3

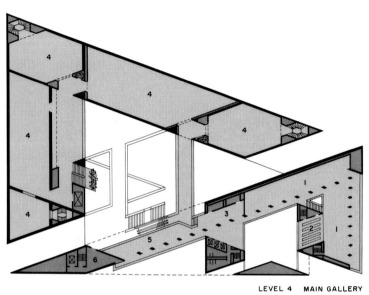

LEVEL 4   MAIN GALLERY

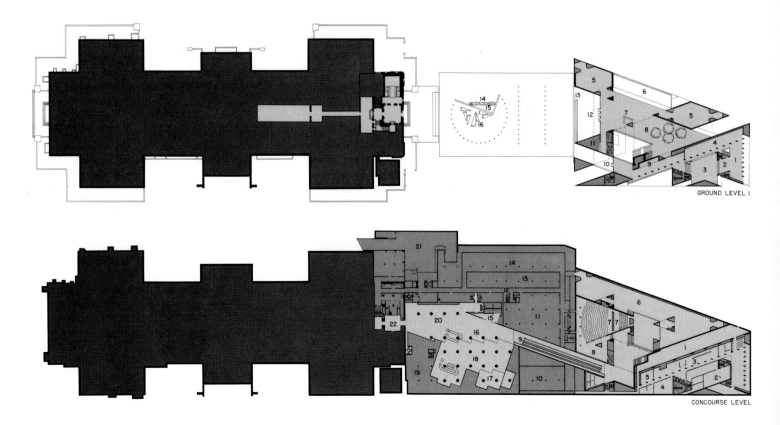

GROUND LEVEL I

CONCOURSE LEVEL

body else, and gave the creature life.

They gave a lot more to the East Building, attentive to the architect's concept. In a period when air supply and air return have been seen to dash about on metabolic binges, this building's air supply and air return are neatly folded into the construction. The respiration is silent. "You *can* express too much," says Mr. Pei. Air comes in not only through those reveals in the marble, but also through the sides of some flush-mounted lights in the ceilings. Air is also brought in through discrete slits along the edges of the bridges and floor levels overlooking the court. Air is returned, as inconspicuously, through reveals tucked under the treads of the stairs, and through openings in the courtyard benches.

This main level, up from the concourse, or in from the Fourth Street entrance, has two gallery areas nestled into Mr. Brown's "houses"—one in the northeast house, one in the northwest house. These towers (all three are parallelograms with spiral stairs or elevators set into their corners) define spaces for exhibition that are hexagonal and, in a few cases, triangular. On the mezzanine level are two more galleries, one presently housing a profusion of Piranesis. There is also a lounge here, and a sales area. The next level can be reached by a balcony-like stair (very Romeo and Juliet) jutting out over the court, above the mezzanine bridge, and this balcony is planted with little lemon trees, which, along with everything planted in and about here, were seen to by landscape architect Dan Kiley. This third-level exhibition area has 20,000 square feet of space. It also has a sculpture terrace overlooking the court. Looking out across it to the east, the second of the two bridges in here swoops across the opposite, eastern area of the space, connecting the galleries on the north edge of the isosceles triangle with the cafe (the Terrace Cafe it is called) on the southern edge.

This is one of the moments in the East Building that is most bracing, indicative of the interlocking nature of the triangles making up the original trapezoid. The cafe, overlooking both the court and the Mall to the south, is positionally part of the right triangle, but spatially it connects with the isosceles courtyard. The ceiling extends out from this pleasant recess, where staff, scholars, and the public meet, creating a sense of continuity that not only joins these distinct, if commonly derived, sections but carries one's view from the galleries out, past the cafe, to the greensward of the Mall. The southwest house of the Gallery picks up on the other two on this level, and on the very top floor, up one more spiral stair, the well (like all of them in these houses) being skylit and embellished with a hanging planter, this southwest house has 1,500 square feet of tightly defined, yet luminous gallery space in a tidy triangular room. Matisse cut-outs hang here.

All of this gallery space—from the lower concourse, where there is also a 442-seat auditorium and a smaller 90-seat lecture hall, to the grand range of the main exhibition level, to that aerie up in the southwest house—can be tuned and retuned by the Gallery's staff—into any geometrical configuration that will most sympathetically set off different kinds of art. This tunability is on the broadest band of curatorial frequencies—from the intimate squared-off spaces that have been set into the hexagonal room of the northeast house's main level (there are small Impressionist paintings in here, from the collection of Alisa Mellon Bruce), to the literal hexagonality of the northwest house's upper level (there are metal sculptures by David Smith in here, giving sonorously silent orations amidst a white Spoleto-style forum with generous, gradual steps rising all around). There is not only horizontal flexibility in these galleries, such as those running between the houses on the upper level, but there is also *vertical* flexibility. The concourse gallery has a variable height of 16 feet in most places, going up to 30 feet beneath the northeastern "house." The main-level galleries have a ten-foot height; the next ones, 14 feet; but the larger third-level areas can be, and are, lowered or raised with great latitude, according to the mood and configuration that suit the art best—as much as 30 feet above the floor. So what Mr. Pei and Mr. Brown have achieved here is a flexibility so genuine that, on any visit, one has the feeling that the galleries, as one is experiencing them right then, have been just like that always. This variable sense of fixity, from room to room, is a notable achievement as seen to by those of staff responsible for designing and installing the exhibits—most especially Hugh Ravenel, the Gallery's wizard in this field.

Perhaps there is something unique to the human consciousness in that whenever we try to think into the future, our thoughts jump into the past. The programming, conceptual nature, and planning of the East Building illustrate this. It has been described as a conservative work (certainly a good deal of the art in here is safely established). It may be—but the conservative impulse in its finest sense is to studiously maximize resources, to save, to innovate sparingly and quietly and with knowledge of previous experience. This is a repository, if (in Mr. Brown's hands) a rambunctious one. Its structural repose is suitable—and maybe therefore "conservative." Within this, though, there can be—there is here—great room for exuberance.

The Center for Advanced Study in the Visual Arts, encased in the right triangle of the East Building, is also an example of this. The library with its six balcony-like levels overlooking a 70-foot-high hall (there are olive trees in here) offers a contemplative reading-and-reference space with more than a tracing of monastic and medieval precedent. This arrangement was Mr. Brown's idea.

One refers to this volume of space in a number of ways. Entry is in from Fourth Street, just south from the main entrance to the court and galleries, whereas the isosceles triangle, as Mr. Pei was explaining, is symmetrically on axis with Mr. Pope's building. The splitting apart of this larger isosceles triangle and the smaller right triangle housing the Center adjusts the over-all composition into a compatible relationship with the Mall. It also allows one, upon entering, to look across the concourse to the courtyard level, just opposite. So while the physical separation is maintained, consciousness of the public is deliberately introduced.

On the Fourth Street side, this split-as-synthesis is pointed up by the most-talked-about architectural corner in memory—a 19-degree razor-edge of marble rising the full height of the building and carrying back along the upper northern wall of the Center to the east. Walking around, just south to the Mall, one notices another knowing gesture. The south wall of glass, instead of being parallel to the mall, is deflecting inward, parallel to the 19-degree angle of the Center's sheer cliff, even as the marble below this deflection as well as those expanses of it above the glass are kept strictly parallel to the Mall. Thus the directionality of this right triangle section is inferred and the angle of its hypotenuse repeated, while at the same time the east-west directionality of the Mall itself is reinforced without excessive reference.

On the uppermost level of this seven-story section is the refectory of the Center, with a terraced view of the Mall, and there are several private dining rooms—all of which has been called jokingly (but justifiably) the best new supper club in the capital. Between the refectory and the new board room is another terrace (there are crab apple trees here). New offices for Mr. Mellon and Mr. Brown are nearby. There are closely cropped views of the area from the terrace—James Renwick's original reddish stone "castle" of The Smithsonian Institution, to the southwest, and a powerful one of the Mall converging on the Hill. The warp and the woof of national experience have been pulled apart and rewoven up here, outside this enclave of administration and scholarship. People from, say, Iowa will always know they are in Washington—not just a museum.

Ieoh Ming Pei paid attention to things which, of late, some architects seem scarcely to mention. He paid attention to proportion. He paid attention to scale. He paid attention to existing buildings and streets and spaces. He paid attention to putting materials and parts together considerately and gracefully and lastingly. He paid attention to all of these things, creating (*because* of them) a building full of allusion to the properties and qualities of humanness and history.

Culture may sometimes appear to be, as Buckminster Fuller has said, the flotsam and the jetsam saying to each other that there should be a law against having any waves. The East Building of the National Gallery of Art is a wave that architecture, and its relationship to the values of culture generally, has very much needed.

THE EAST BUILDING OF THE NATIONAL GALLERY OF ART, Washington, D.C. Architects: *I. M. Pei & Partners.* Engineers: *Weiskopf & Pickworth (structural); Syska & Hennessy (mechanical/electrical).* Consultants: *Malcolm Rice (marble); Kiley, Tyndall, Walker (landscape architects).* Construction manager: *Carl Morse, Morse/Diesel, Inc.* Builder: *Chas. H. Tomkins Co.*

VISUAL ARTS CENTER, BOWDOIN COLLEGE

There are some buildings which could only be the way they are—or so they appear. Every choice that went into their making seems to have been inevitable, correct, allowing no alternatives. Edward Larrabee Barnes' Visual Arts Center is such a building. One can imagine ways other fine architects might have added a wing to this particular McKim, Mead and White building on this particular campus— because of course Barnes' solution is not really the only one possible. But it shows his special ability to find solutions for complex problems which seem altogether simple and right.

124

"The old campus of Bowdoin College is even prettier than Harvard Yard" says Edward Larrabee Barnes. He is an architect for whom words like "pretty" come naturally and whose own work calls forth words like "graceful" and "elegant." When Barnes talks about the Visual Arts Center at Bowdoin he has little to say about its cost, mechanical system, structure, acoustics, lighting—aspects of the building which nonetheless clearly consumed his attention because they are so well resolved. An engineer and cost accountant by necessity, he is nonetheless an architect who thinks and feels like an artist. He prefers to talk about his search for the kind of symmetry, proportion, mass and scale for the Visual Arts Center which would be in harmony with the buildings that surround it.

As an artist first and foremost, Barnes belongs in the company of the great architects who have built on the oldest quadrangle of the campus. They are the Neo-Classicists McKim, Mead and White who designed the Colonial-Revival Walker Art Museum which the Visual Arts Center adjoins, and the Romanticist Richard Upjohn whose Early American Gothic Revival chapel the Visual Arts Center axially confronts.

The Walker Art Museum is similar in design to one of McKim, Mead and White's masterpieces, the Morgan Library in New York and is a beautiful building in its own right. It has the same Palladian references as the Morgan. Both the Walker and the Morgan are entered through a *serliana,* or loggia derived from Palladio's Basilica in Vicenza and both are graced by a dome. Barnes was originally requested by Bowdoin to design the proposed Visual Arts Center as a wing added to the symmetrically perfect Walker. He indeed made the connection—but invisibly, underground.

Richard Upjohn's simple, picturesque and rustic stone chapel at Bowdoin is one of the oldest buildings on the campus. It is on axis with the main gate. The path from the chapel across the quadrangle and through the gate is a ceremonial passage for the graduating class and for wedding and funeral processions. Barnes' new building bridges the path.

The old quadrangle itself is filled with ancient elms and covered by a canopy of branches and leaves. It is defined by buildings of congenial height and massing, separated from each other by distances roughly equal to their lengths. It is a fine campus of the kind only to be found in the United States and not at all similar to the closed quadrangles of Oxford and Cambridge or universities on the Continent.

"I love this campus," says Barnes. "The buildings make the quadrangle seem like a great room, but because so much space is squandered between each building you can look through it in all directions. Originally I was expected to hook the new building onto the McKim, Mead and White structure. I insisted that it had to be one more separate building and not a wing, to respect the open-close, open-close perimeter of the quadrangle.

"I am told that I should feel guilty for always creating symmetrical buildings, but this time I have no guilt. Symmetry was absolutely essential. The formal balance of the Visual Arts Center conforms to the classicism of the Walker Art Museum, but the real reason for the symmetry was the necessary placement of the building on the axial path bisecting the main gate to the campus at one end and the Upjohn chapel doorway at the other.

"My big decision was to design the Visual Arts Center around a daylighted, unheated walk-through space that preserves and enhances the ceremonial walk. Le Corbusier's Carpenter Center at Harvard is the first building I ever saw where a campus walk is taken through and out again. On your way you can see the students at work through the glass walls. I knew that something like it would work at Bowdoin."

As the plans indicate, the walk-through opening fans out almost at once, echoing the diagonal campus walks and allowing a wide yet framed view of the quadrangle during the brief passage through the building. The walk-through is completely open in good weather, but can be closed in winter by an ingenious system of custom-made wooden doors. These are the most complex of the building's many elegant details designed by Barnes' associate Alistair Bevington.

As can be seen on the site plan (below) the facade facing the quadrangle lines up exactly with the facade of the Walker Art Center, the projections of Gibson Hall and the setback of the Searles Building. Thus Barnes respects the long-established perimeter of his side of the quadrangle.

The cornice of the Visual Arts Center lines up with the underside of the cornice of the McKim, Mead and White building. Barnes made the width and depth of his building roughly the same as that of the Walker, so that "these two blocks as masses seen in moonlight without detail would share the same density, the same stance."

The facade which faces the main campus gate (below) has a high studio window as wide as the entrance to the walk-through. Its width in turn is established by the distance between the Doric columns of the gate. The austere shapes and elegant proportions of the high window and the entrance below, juxtaposed against the ornamental columns, form a campus entrance of great subtlety and sophistication.

The Visual Arts Center is easily recognized as a work of Barnes and no one else. What makes it so unmistakeably his, however, can not be explained by his method of problem solving as he describes it. Although Barnes' attempts to explain his buildings tell us very much about them, they also tell us very little, for like most architects he does not talk about the way his work expresses his nature, nor may he have much of an idea how it does.

Since Barnes is an architect who is also an artist his work must indeed express his nature. His buildings seem to be the work of a spirit which rejects the spontaneous, the accidental, the capricious and the unessential, and thereby achieves an architecture of great reticence and repose.

VISUAL ARTS CENTER. Bowdoin College, Brunswick, Maine. Architect: *Edward Larrabee Barnes—associate: Alistair Bevington; project architect: Demetri Sarantitis.* Consultants: *Zoldos-Silman (structural); Hannaham & Johnson (mechanical); Donald Bliss (lighting); Nicholas Quennell (landscape); Donald Wolf and Company (costs).* General contractor: *Davison Construction Corp.*

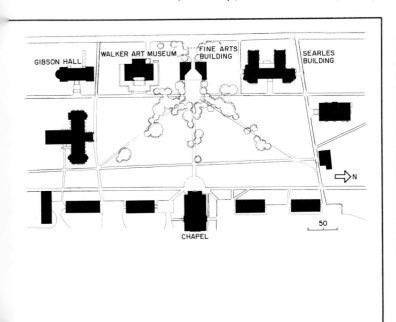

Edward Larrabee Barnes

The plan of the old quadrangle (preceding page) shows the axial relationship between the Visual Arts Center and the Richard Upjohn chapel (left). On the opposite page is the entrance gate facade. Shown above are views of the Walker Art Museum, and the Searles Building. Because Barnes believes that the individual buildings that define the quadrangle are in very good scale to each other, he made the Visual Art Center approximately similar in size and massing. Above ground and visible are three stories, the first containing classrooms, the second a library and offices and the third a high-ceilinged, skylit studio. Other spaces are below ground (right). A new lawn has been created above ground.

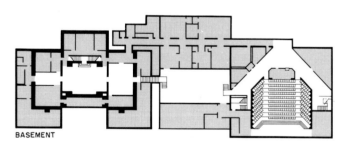
BASEMENT

The basement plan shows the underground link between the Visual Arts Center and the Walker Art Museum. The shaded areas indicate offices and workshops. A new gallery links the museum galleries with the new auditorium and stage. The Y-shape echoes the walk-through at the ground level above. The auditorium, gallery and student workshops beneath the brick paving and lawn are roofed over with exposed long-span, precast concrete tees. The all concrete structure stops at grade where the steel-frame superstructure begins.

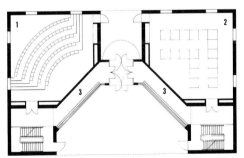

FIRST FLOOR

1. Eighty-seat classroom
2. Picture study room
3. Gallery

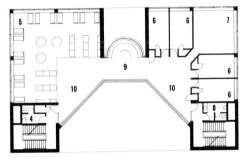

SECOND FLOOR

4. Women's room
5. Library
6. Office
7. Seminar
8. Men's room
9. Lounge
10. Secretarial

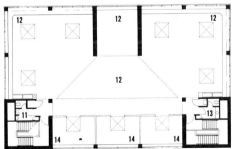

THIRD FLOOR

11. Men's room
12. Studio
13. Women's room
14. Private studios

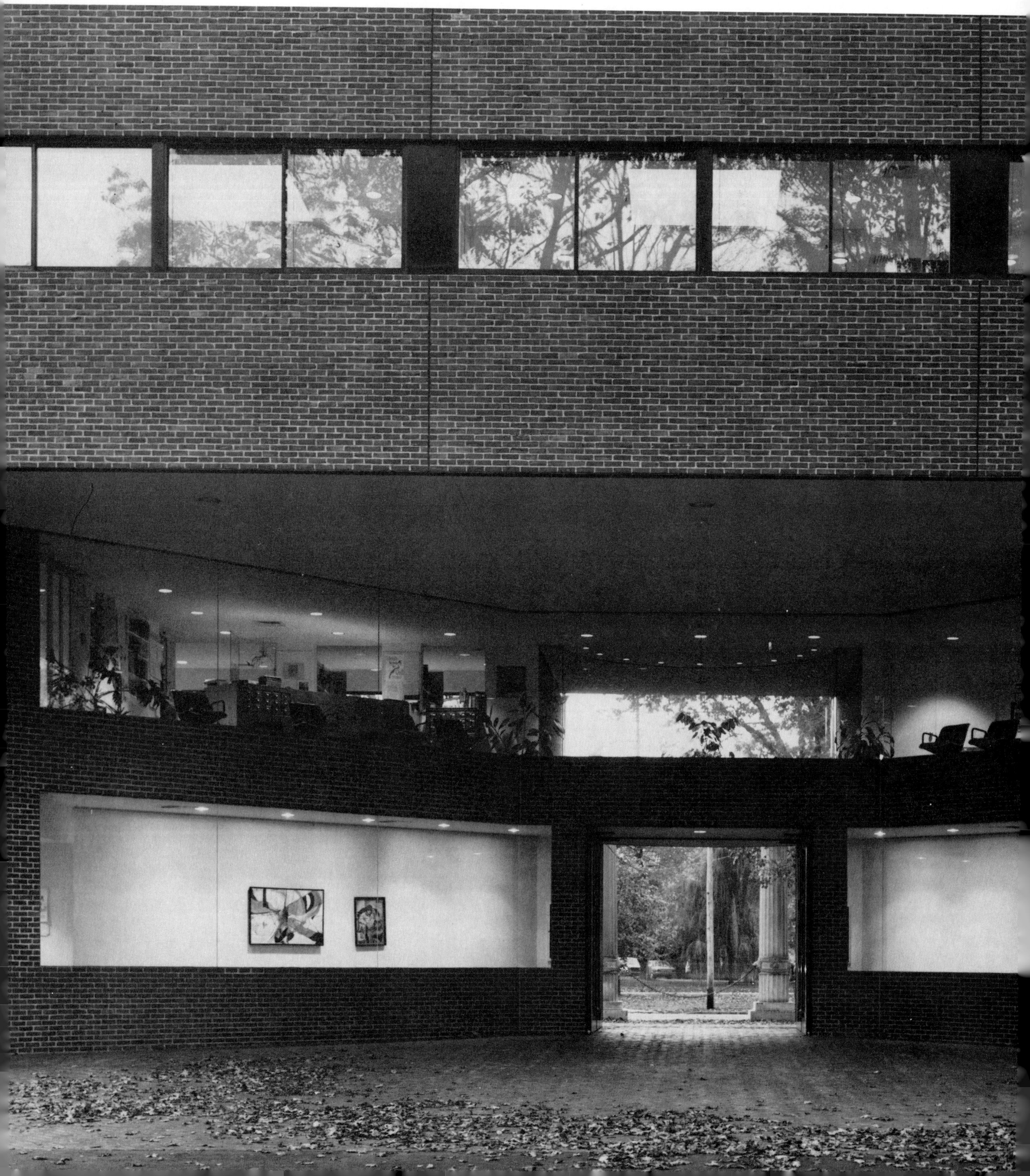

The proportions of the Visual Arts Center appear to be generated by Barnes' intuition rather than by any mathematical formulas. His vocabulary of materials and forms is austere, but paradoxically the building seems almost luxurious because of its superb detailing. The brick is used in three ways—in a herring bone pattern on the ground, a running bond for the walls and in a soldier course to help articulate the semi-circular curve of the library lounge (above). The lounge is glazed on both sides increasing the transparency of the opening. The deep overhangs and old trees shield the interiors from glare. The paintings in the gallery space to the left and right of the walk-through announce the building's function as an art center and bring the vibrancy of contemporary artistic life to the 19th-century quadrangle.

129

130

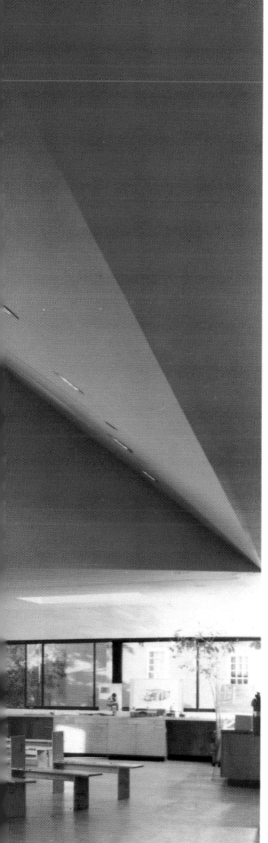

The dramatic height of the centered studio window, which on the exterior so dramatically reinforces the entrance to the Visual Arts Center and the campus beyond, enhances the main studio (left) as well. The Y-shape used in the basement and the first and second floors of the structure also appears as a ceiling form on the studio floor. It becomes a tilted trapezoid which makes the transition from the high ceilinged rectangular volume at the window to the lower ceiling of the surrounding studio. Beyond this trapezoidal hood, the studios are well lit by skylights. The main studio is one big flexible space with ample windows shaded by the huge elm trees which surround it. The perimeter wall of the studio is lined with storage cabinets under a continuous work ledge at the window sill.

131

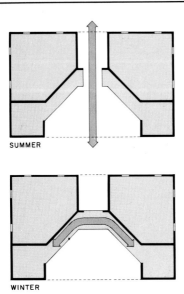

SUMMER

WINTER

The water-struck wood-fired "Eno" brick is from the same lot used by Louis Kahn on his Exeter College Library in New Hampshire. It is close in texture and color to brick in the adjoining Walker Museum. The large areas of fixed glazing on the walk-through (above) increase the transparency of the building in both directions on the chapel axis. The second floor is the most transparent. From the library lounge (above) the paired Doric columns of the entry gate are visible through the glass semi-circle looking west. The lounge has uninterrupted glazing to the east as well opening up the view to the quadrangle and chapel. The specially designed doors (right) pivot to close the passage in winter. This detail was difficult to work out. The success of the entire concept, however, depended upon the correct design and construction of these doors.

If the Visual Arts Center were sited on a treeless plain it would not satisfy us as completely as it does planted here among Bowdoin's stately elms. A denial of nature and the ornament derived from it is part of what abstract architecture and painting are about. Piet Mondrian never faced the sidewalk when sitting in a cafe because he did not wish to look at the people and trees. People who live in rational, abstract spaces, however, tend to fill them with plants, and buildings purified of ornament and caprice tend to look better among trees. Barnes' building looks wonderful at Bowdoin, but in this instance it is no accident of nature. Barnes designed the Visual Arts Center so that the elms would be its ornament. From inside, framed by the huge windows they are living wall decoration. Outside they shadow, dapple and soften the plain brick surfaces.

AIA NATIONAL HEADQUARTERS BUILDING

Ask an architect if a given handsome, historic, landmark building and its garden should be preserved and he would say: "If at all possible, yes." To the question as to whether one can design a contemporary structure which would effectively blend with a notable building of bygone style, he would reply: "Certainly." If pressed to recommend how this could best be done, he might very well say: "Hold a competition!" Finally, if asked how best to make sure that the competition winning scheme would respect the landmark and its neighborhood, he would add: "There should be a disinterested board of review with power to accept or reject."

In the problems inherent in expanding their Washington headquarters, the American Institute of Architects made three fundamental decisions—each of which reflects the foregoing beliefs and aspirations of the typical architect, and a final decision reflecting the necessary pragmatism of the profession. First, they decided to preserve the historic and beautiful Octagon and its garden; second, they held a competition for the design of a new headquarters building to share the site and be in harmony with the landmark; third, with some chagrin they deferred to a series of rejections by Washington, D.C.'s Fine Arts Commission (which the AIA helped create) of the winning design and modifications thereof; fourth, they faced the necessity of accepting the resignation of the competition winning firm and selected another architectural firm by a method other than holding a formal competition.

The results would appear to be the very best that architects designing for themselves can do. By living up to their own highest standards and practicing what they preach, the architectural profession has not only enhanced the Washington landscape, but it has created the physical framework for projecting a continuously effective image for itself.

The radial axes of Major Pierre L'Enfant's plan for Washington, D.C. shaped the non-rectangular corner which the Octagon House, designed in 1798 by William Thornton, turns so elegantly. One hundred and seventy five years later, architects Norman Fletcher and Howard Elkus of TAC completed the composition.
The events which led to their commission to design the new AIA National Headquarters Building, and the considerations which influenced their final design were complex and difficult, but the results are distinguished.

The history
of the project

In 1960, the AIA Committee on the Profession cited "the pressures of a growing membership and the increasing numbers of jobs to be done for the profession" as reasons for building a new national headquarters. The existing headquarters then included the Octagon House and an administration building beyond the garden which had been constructed in 1941 and incorporated the old stables on the site. A "New Headquarters Building Committee" was formed whose members were: Hugh A. Stubbins, Jr. FAIA, William L. Pereira, FAIA, and Arthur G. Odell, Jr., FAIA. Its chairman was Leon Chatelain, Jr. FAIA.

This committee decided that further vertical expansion of the administration wing was unfeasible from both a structural and architectural standpoint and that horizontal expansion would encroach upon the garden and call for extensive and costly additional land acquisition. After examining the possibility of moving the AIA headquarters out of Washington, the committee concluded that to be effective, politically and symbolically, the AIA headquarters should remain in the capital.

The committee, aided by the architectural firm of Satterlee and Smith, and with the help of a real estate consultant, examined the Octagon House site in terms of the prestige inherent in its proximity to the White House, the presence of a cherished landmark, and the economics of preserving and maintaining the latter. Research confirmed that the landmark would be hard to sell, but on the

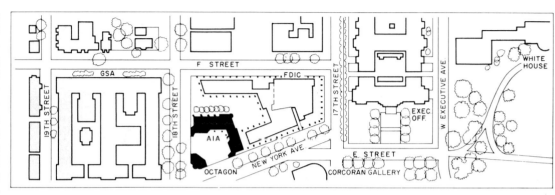

other hand, the land itself had an equity value of almost $1 million for building on the site. Other sites in Washington were studied from many standpoints. The advantages, however, continued to lie with the present site, even though preserving the Octagon House would make the design of the new headquarters more complicated and difficult. Not the least of the difficulties which could be foreseen was the fact that additions adjacent to the Octagon House, as a registered National Historic Landmark in an area of the District of Columbia over which the Fine Arts Commission has review authority, would be suspect to approval by this body.

In 1963 the "New Headquarters Building Committee" was disbanded and a new group with a slightly different title was formed. The new members of the "New Headquarters Committee" were: Robert F. Hastings, FAIA, Henry L. Wright, FAIA, and chairman Charles M. Nes, Jr., FAIA. Stubbins and Chatelain continued to serve. Because the AIA membership had

voted that the architect for the new building should be selected by competition, late in 1963 a jury was selected. Stubbins agreed to serve along with Edward L. Barnes, AIA, J. Roy Carroll, FAIA, O'Neil Ford, FAIA and John Carl Warnecke, FAIA.

The competition program charged the prospective competitors with ". . . the creation of a design for a new National Headquarters Building that will satisfy both physical and spiritual functions—a building of special architectural significance, establishing a symbol of the creative genius of our time yet complementing, protecting and preserving a cherished symbol of another time, the historic Octagon House."

Winners of the two-stage competition were Mitchell/Giurgola Associates. Their winning design (fig. 1), announced in November 1964, featured a semi-circular, concave glass wall as the background for the Octagon House. Within the next two years, however, the AIA voted to renovate the Octagon House, purchase

the adjacent Lemon Building and redesign the proposed headquarters structure for 130,000 feet of floor space in contrast to the 80,000 called for in the competition.

Mitchell/Giurgola Associates prepared a new design (fig. 2) embodying the change in size. It differed in other ways from the competition winning design. The concave glass facade was gone and in its place were two vertically-walled floors at the base and five additional floors projecting forward over the garden in a series of reverse steps. At the rear of the building these five floors were enclosed by a slanted skylight.

A number of architects who reviewed the design feared that its cost would exceed the $30 per square foot that had been budgeted for the building. They received support from an unexpected quarter, on different grounds, when the Fine Arts Commission declared the design "out of keeping with the feeling of the Octagon" and rejected it. William Walton, Gordon Bunshaft and the

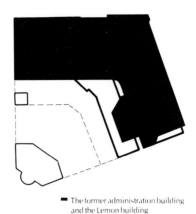

The former administration building and the Lemon building

By building to the maximum allowable building height of 90 feet (and thus blocking out adjoining buildings) a continuous backdrop for the Octagon was created.

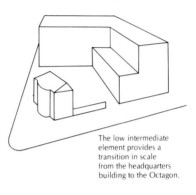

The low intermediate element provides a transition in scale from the headquarters building to the Octagon.

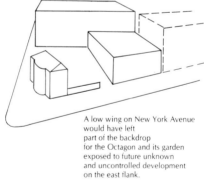

A low wing on New York Avenue would have left part of the backdrop for the Octagon and its garden exposed to future unknown and uncontrolled development on the east flank.

To create a successful scale relationship between the Octagon and the new headquarters building, it was necessary to maximize the distance between them. Further, this maximum distance increases the availability of southern light for the garden.

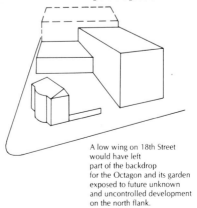

A low wing on 18th Street would have left part of the backdrop for the Octagon and its garden exposed to future unknown and uncontrolled development on the north flank.

other Commission members stated that the proposed design overwhelmed its elegant neighbor and reiterated their belief that the new building should be a quiet backdrop for the Octagon House.

Robert L. Durham, FAIA, then president of the AIA, stated for the record that the Institute's "belief in the need for the Fine Arts Commission and comparable design review boards throughout the country" led it to defer to the Commission's rejection and try again. Mitchell/Giurgola Associates produced still another design (fig. 3). In this design the height of the building was reduced, the set back from the Octagon House was increased and the floors were stacked vertically in the conventional way. A controversial design feature was the "notch" at the intersection of the two wings.

Once more the design was formally submitted to the Fine Arts Commission and this time, still under the influence of Bunshaft, the Commission balked at the notch and again rejected the building. Mitchell/Giurgola Associates refused to further compromise their design by restudying the notch and in September 1968, they resigned. By then George Kassabaum, FAIA, was president of the Institute, and he reiterated the principle that design review boards were "the best known means of maintaining order in the face of all of the pressures leading to chaos."

The AIA then proceeded to reorder the chaos into which its headquarters program had now fallen by appointing then-board member Max O. Urbahn, FAIA, to chair a committee to figure out what to do next. In December 1968 Urbahn recommended that a committee of architects be organized to select an architect. The board appointed Rex W. Allen, FAIA, Edward Charles Bassett, AIA, Romaldo Giurgola, AIA, G. Harold W. Haag, FAIA, Morris Ketchum, Jr. FAIA, Willis N. Mills, FAIA, I. M. Pei, FAIA and Philip Will Jr., FAIA. Urbahn agreed to be chairman. This committee proceeded to interview architects and finally selected Norman C. Fletcher of The Architects Collaborative to design the building. The latter chose TAC senior associate Howard F. Elkus to work with him on the project. Under Urbahn's leadership a series of informal meetings were held between TAC and the Fine Arts Commission during the design process. The formal approval went without a hitch, the funds were voted and the mortgage arranged.

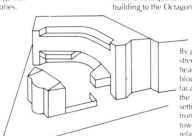

The terrace cutback on the seventh floor of the headquarters building reduces the apparent height from the garden facade to six stories.

The curved facade eliminates the appearance of separate wings or a central corner, and stresses the continuity and flow of the building around the garden from one street to the other.

The diagonal masses, elements and lines of force visually link the headquarters building to the Octagon.

The old garden walls of the Octagon were rebuilt to link the Octagon with the new headquarters building and enclose the garden. The return of the wall at the New York Avenue entrance, and the old smokehouse at the 18th street entrance form zones of transition from these streets to the garden.

The projecting elements of the board room and executive suite recall the Octagon mass but are subordinate in height and size.

By partially recessing the street facade of the headquarters building, the block long mass of adjoining facades is interrupted and the building in its special setting is thus distinguished from its neighbors. The stair towers have been designed to relate to the geometry and massing of the Octagon while at the same time turning the corner.

The recess at the third story lightens the apparent mass of the office floors thus ameliorating and rendering more sympathetic the scale relationships between the headquarters building and the Octagon.

TAC's approach to the design of the building

Architects Fletcher and Elkus first made a feasibility study and plan for the redevelopment of the entire block (fig. 4). At the time a new Federal Deposit Insurance Company Building had been constructed at the end of the block opposite the Octagon House, but the area in between was occupied by a parking lot, an old hospital, townhouses and an office building. This TAC preliminary plan provided a central plaza between the proposed AIA building and the FDIC. The plaza would have had open arcades and several entrances from the adjoining streets. It was hoped that this provision of open space would have led to a

rezoning of building heights and densities to make the plaza economically feasible to prospective developers. The new headquarters building was to have opened directly on to the plaza, although the main entrance was, as now, on the garden side facing the Octagon.

As it turned out, the AIA was unable to achieve joint block planning. The developer of the hospital site replaced that building with one that extended to the AIA property line and deep into the center of the block, and the owners of the property on 18th street also maximized the use of their site. TAC, accordingly, eliminated the plans for an entrance and plaza at the rear of the building toward the center of the block.

The design
as built

The form of the new headquarters building (figs. 5, 6, 7, 8, 9) derived mainly from the requirement that as much space as possible be given to the Octagon House and its garden, while minimizing the scale of the new building. To this end the building utilizes considerably less square footage than the amount permitted by the local zoning. The principal access to the headquarters is through the plaza which is open to the sun and quite pleasant to walk through.

By extending continuous glass walls up to the third floor TAC has given the building the appearance of having been hollowed out, and thus it seems to draw back from the Octagon House. Elements which are smaller in scale than the Octagon House have been emphasized for contrast and balance. The conference room projects forward and its concrete walls contrast effectively with the glass facade (fig. 10). This element helps define the main entrance and shelters arriving visitors. The executive wing has been separately articulated as a scale transition.

The building is 90 feet high which is the maximum permitted in Washington, D.C. It was essential that the building be designed to this height in order to screen the neighboring buildings constructed on the AIA property line, especially as it became certain that these would be built to the maximum height. The top floor of the headquarters building is set back so that from all vantage points close to the building there appear to be six, rather than seven floors—another effective scale reducing device.

TAC's efforts to create as simple a backdrop for the Octagon House as possible prompted them to unite the north and east wings in a strong continuous curve that frames the garden. The interior organization of the building derives from this curve and the distinctive geometry of the site (fig. 11). The sweep of the building and the vectors of the site are combined in angled spaces, closer to the angles of a hexagon than those of a rectangle. These echo the angles of the Octagon House which is actually six-sided. Norman Fletcher likes to cite Frank Lloyd Wright's Hanna House in California as proof that such spaces flow more easily than 90 degree spaces. A triangulated ceiling system designed within this geometry which was an integrated structural, mechanical, electrical and com-

munications sandwich (August 1970, page 46) was abandoned because of cost and replaced by a conventional acoustical grid ceiling which is suspended from a single coffered slab.

The two ends of the building have been designed as simple shafts which incorporate the necessary stair towers. Their uninterrupted surfaces terminate the long sweep of the windows within the curve of the headquarters building (fig. 12). These towers also terminate the vistas down New York Avenue (fig. 13) and 18th Street, forming a two-sided frame for the Octagon House.

The original brick walls of the Octagon House and garden have been extended and refurbished. The old smokehouse, moved for a time during the construction, has been replaced in its original location. The original wooden gates of the property have also been restored. The brick sidewalks around the site have been relaid and repaired and the brick garden walks have been extended onto the larger terrace. This brick paving extends from the terrace into the ground floor exhibition area, thus integrating the old spaces and materials with the new.

TAC believes the other materials in the new building to be in sympathy with the Octagon House. The grey precast concrete relates well to the dark brick of the historic structure. Most importantly, the clear glass of the first two floors enables people outside to see the activity and the displays within.

The spatial organization within the building is as follows: two large underground floors house the garage, such services as printing and accounting, and mechanical equipment; the first three floors above ground are for AIA use, including the public exhibition space; and the top four floors are for tenants.

A new environment
for the AIA

Of most concern to TAC was the concept of the new AIA headquarters as a place where architects from all parts of the country will feel at home and like to return to. So far, members who have visited the new building are reacting positively. Norman Fletcher has noted with some pride that "the people of Washington cross the plaza on their walks. Already they enjoy the Octagon House and the garden. Soon they will see lively exhibits related to the arts, architecture and urban planning dis-

played in the exhibition hall and the adjoining plaza. We hope to have been successful in our attempt to design a building which provides for the daily needs of the profession *and* gives something back to the city."

AIA NATIONAL HEADQUARTERS BUILDING, Washington, D.C. Architects: *The Architects Collaborative—principal-in-charge: Norman C. Fletcher; senior-associate-in-charge: Howard F. Elkus; job captains: James F. Armstrong, John E. Wyman; landscape designers: Knox C. Johnson, Hugh T. Kirkley; interiors: Ann G. Elwell; architects' representative: Richard T. Malesardi. Engineers: LeMessurier Associates, Inc. (structural); Cosentini Associates, Inc. (mechanical); Bolt, Beranek & Newman, Inc. (acoustical); Golder, Gass Associates (soil). General contractor: The Volpe Construction Company, Inc.*

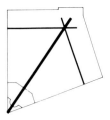

■ The bisector of the intersecting perpendiculars to the angled streets shapes the basic geometry of the design solution

The 175 year-old Octagon occupies
the corner of a triangular site at the
juncture of New York Avenue and 18th
~~~~~~~~ D.C. The garden
~~~~~~~~~~~~~~ is slightly
~~~~~~~~~~~~~~ new head-
~~~~~~~~~~~~~ apped around
~~~~~~~~~~~~ ground floor plan
~~~~~~ bird's-eye photo (below)
indicate, a broad curving plaza forms
a pedestrian path, open to the public,
which connects the intersecting streets.
The architects—Norman Fletcher and
Howard Elkus of The Architects Collaborative—conceived the plaza as an
extension of the garden, paved it in red
brick to match the old brick in the re-
constructed garden paths, and extended this brick into the ground floor
exhibition space of the new structure.
Conceived as a "background building," the new headquarters permits the
Octagon House to dominate (left).

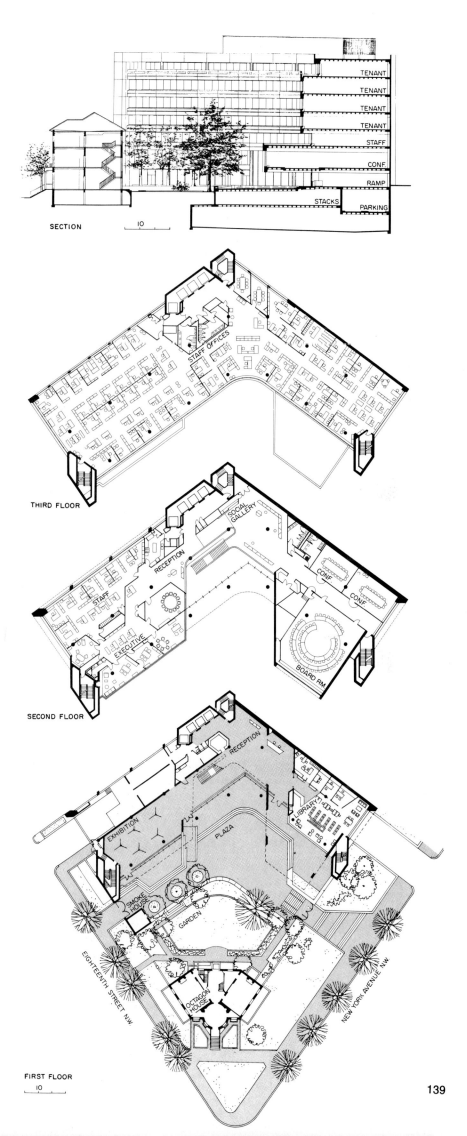

SECTION

THIRD FLOOR

SECOND FLOOR

FIRST FLOOR

139

To walk about the AIA's new headquarters is to sense that the building is correct, right, and designed as it should be. From the lobby mezzanine (left and above) one looks down into the ground floor exhibition space and across the plaza to the Octagon and its garden. Together the latter have become the focus of the composition, playing the same role in space that a fountain, or gazebo or pavilion does in the context of other scales. Because of skillful massing, the new building, in spite of its size, does not appear to crowd the landmark. At present the transition between the plaza and garden is gentle. As the new trees grow larger the integration of the two spaces will continue to improve. The generous exhibition gallery (below), in conjunction with the broad plaza affords the AIA the opportunity to mount combined indoor and outdoor displays to further the public interest in architecture and the environment. The prominent location of their headquarters, within a short walk from the White House, should bring many visitors to the AIA's exhibits, provided they are frequent, well done and well publicized.

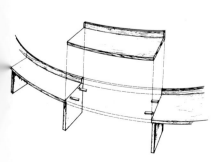

The offices of the president of the AIA (top left) and the executive vice president (bottom left) overlook the plaza and the Octagon and its garden. The spatial arrangement of the vice president's office is particularly efficient and attractive because of the skillful way in which the room is divided into deskwork, conference and reading areas. The conference center (above) projects out over the plaza. It has been designed to accommodate a full range of audio-visual aids. The circular desks can be disassembled and rearranged or stored as shown in the detail (left). Open planning is used throughout the general offices and the system of partitioning consists of commercially available storage units surfaced in white laminated plastic (right).

DIXWELL
FIRE
STATION

Venturi and Rauch's Dixwell Fire Station is a splendid building entirely on its own—surreal in the positive, literal sense of being super-real, as real as your corner gas station, and as super as you would feel as a ten-year-old at the wheel of a speeding American LaFrance hook-and-ladder, siren howling, dalmatians close behind. Before getting carried away by the building, however, we must remember to talk about *context,* which is supposedly the key to understanding these pesky "inclusivists," with their tiresome insistence on recognizing the existence of buildings other than their own.

In the case of New Haven, which shares with Columbus, Indiana, the distinction of being either the showcase or the elephants' burying ground of modern American architecture, there is a heap o' context.

One of the earliest critics of New Haven's architecture was a visitor from the Massachusetts Bay Colony, who observed that, given the settlement's modest size and wealth, its houses were perhaps overly "elaborate." Indeed, New Haven was one of North America's first planned cities, designed to be the capital of a large, independent colony. Through a series of economic and political misadventures, however, this role was never fulfilled. The city found its true identity as a solid, lower-middle class, ethnically diverse factory town like many others in New England, passing in and out of the fiscal doldrums unto the present day. Its original pretensions, however, kept alive by the presence of Yale University, were never forgotten. In this way the city developed a kind of architectural split personality. Generations of snobbish Yalies observed that if it were not for Yale, New Haven would be Bridgeport—a saying so old that it might have been attributed to that visitor from Massachusetts, had Bridgeport and Yale existed at the time.

In their search for built grandeur, Yale and New Haven have almost always opted for the exotic and the richly eclectic. It is a taste shared by other, deceptively conservative New England towns, in whose squalid, damp climate the latest gewgaw just off the India clipper often made better architecture than the masterly, correct, and magnificent play of forms in the murk. New Haven's native architect laureate, Henry Austin, in the mid-19th century honed his taste to a fine edge of insanity with his Moorish-Gothic-Italianate villas, sprouting enough cupolas, overhangs, and brackets to make Frank Furness look like Walter Gropius. Later, having torn down its original door, the Harvardesque Brick Row, Yale imported a long series of architectural carpetbaggers to create, among other things, a building that is Gothic in front and Georgian in back, and an intersection whose four corners contain Gothic, Georgian, Venetian, and Moorish buildings respectively. (The Moorish one, a secret society by Richard Morris Hunt, is hard by an enormous Beaux-Arts facade by Carrére and Hastings, which is in turn across the street from Austin's Egyptian cemetery gate and the world's largest Gothic power plant.)

Coexisting, more or less, with all this was the other New Haven: three-decker houses on elm-lined streets, open-air markets, scattered factory loft buildings, lots of Queen Anne porches and Jane Jacobean amenities as well as a few genuine, unpicturesque slums. Never exactly prosperous, this New Haven was hit hard after World War II by the now-familiar inner-city problems, including rampant suburbanization.

It was the rise of the cities, the car culture and the highway programs, and the invention in the early 1950s of urban renewal that finally, after three hundred years, allowed dons and burghers led by Mayor Richard C. Lee to drive a wedge both literal and figurative between the fantastic, pinnacled, and towered dream capital and its grubby industrial underpinnings. The wedge was the Oak Street Connector, a six-lane highway which even now connects nothing, but which was then seen as a way to bring suburbanites into the city to shop at Chapel Square, a brand new, poisonously dull downtown version of a suburban shopping center, and as the first link in a projected ring road, a carbon monoxide moat between the official fantasyland and the racial and ethnic minorities on its fringes. The connector and related projects displaced thousands of low-income residents, many of whom had no alternative but to leave the city: New Haven, it was now said, looked like Bridgeport because much of New Haven was *in* Bridgeport.

This and other abuses of urban renewal in New Haven, as elsewhere, led in a short time to one of the sincerest forms of environmental criticism—rioting—and a reluctant general admission that something was wrong, followed in a few years by the Nixonian dismantling of the whole renewal machine.

In the meantime, a remarkable collection of buildings had been produced on the Yale campus and elsewhere throughout the city center. Like the story of New Haven's urban renewal process, the story of these buildings is well enough known to anyone interested enough in architectural journalism to get past the sauna ads. While impressed by the extreme originality of, say, Saarinen's hockey rink or Bunshaft's rare book library, some critics demurred that these buildings bore almost no relationship to their surroundings. We have just seen, however, that by encouraging stubborn discontinuity of style and a taste for the grandly exotic, these architects were following in well-trodden paths. Mayor Lee's innovations were confined to speed, scale of execution and completion, and space. Great spaces—sometimes "plazas" but usually parking lots—often denied the city one compensating benefit of its cacophony of styles: the nutty, accidental charm of their close juxtaposition.

It is not surprising that many in New Haven, including many architects, were politically radicalized by the worst excesses of the renewal years. It is a bit surprising, or at least ironic, that in these same years a thoughtful critique of urban renewal's way of building emerged at Yale (which became in these years the northern outpost of something called the "New Haven-Philadelphia Axis," apparently a sort of DEW line for intercepting Miesian propaganda being lobbed over from Chicago).

The architects who developed this critique, either written or built or both, were all in some way students of Louis I. Kahn, influenced by Vincent Scully, and destined later to be called "inclusivists." Their main arguments against the renewal mentality and the accompanying antisepsis of knee-jerk Modernism, and in favor of the messy, difficult vitality of the existing environment dealt with on its own terms, are by now so current that even Ulrich Franzen can claim to be complex and contradictory and get away with it.

It is worth remembering, however, that in 1966, when *Complexity and Contradiction in Architecture* was published, urban renewal was an article of faith, and that when Robert Venturi said that "Main Street is almost all right," his statement was seen not so much as radical, but as purely incomprehensible. In his introduction, however, Vincent Scully made his own view of the matter (in Philip Johnson's phrase) bludgeon-like clear: "[Venturi's] proposals, in their recognition of complexity and their respect for what exists, create the most necessary antidote to that cataclysmic purism of contemporary urban renewal which has presently brought so many cities to the brink of catastrophe."

I happen to agree with that statement. Scully, however, never one to linger long in the grey middle areas of opinion, tempts me to continue in the mode of the good guys against the bad guys. What, my readers now ask breathlessly, happened then? We know that urban renewal bit the dust, so Venturi and the other inclusivists must have won, right? Socked the old antidote right in there. Stuffed Gordon Bunshaft into the Fine Arts Commission's gingerbread oven and lived happily ever after.

Unfortunately, this was not the case. Renewal programs were rescinded in general, as part of a new political and economic retreat from the cities, a conservative reaction to the fact that Federal largesse had, incredibly as it seemed, been met with riots and resentment. The new "respect for what exists," then, was often highly pragmatic. For not a few architects, preservationism, "ad hocism," adaptive re-use, recycling, and "context" represented a bandwagon loaded with sour grapes.

In New Haven, the mood is less one of resentful pragmatism than of exhaustion, a return to economic standstill in the aftermath of the renewal bonanza. Few opportunities exist for any kind of building, but, if they did, there is little evidence that the Yale Corporation and the City Fathers, supposedly having learned their lesson, would now ask their architects to study the restoring of the Chapel Street five and ten cent stores and black storefront churches in the Hill in preparation for doing things better next time. There is every reason to suspect, on the contrary, that the habits of three hundred years are not easily broken, and that New Haven is simply waiting for a break to go architecturally bananas once again.

Out of this, Robert Venturi and the firm of Venturi and Rauch have gotten one small opportunity, the Dixwell Fire Station, to demonstrate their alternative (the firm's well-known, competition-winning project for the Yale Mathematics Building is apparently stalled for lack of funds). And, in some respects, the building does not seem to represent an alternative at all. It is clearly a special, unusual build-ing; to anyone attuned to such things, as many New Haveners are, it has visible pretensions to high art—the extending fin wall, for example. One might suspect the involvement of yet another in the long tradition of out-of-town, Yale-connected architects. This is in fact true.

But it is not the purpose of this, or any other Venturi and Rauch building, to look *precisely* ordinary, to imitate, in this case, one of the nearby auto body shops, as if on a movie set. What the firehouse tried to do instead, with considerable success, is to be both a special, even monumental public building, *and at the same time* to be part of the factory town of New Haven, as the garages of automobile row so clearly are. To the extent to which it succeeds in doing this, Venturi and Rauch's small building, symbolically located on the border between Yale's turf and the black Dixwell neighborhood (and very near the proposed site of the dividing ring road), rejoins the halves of the city's dual identity, grandiose fantasy and grubby reality. It is very nearly the first Modern building of any architectural ambition to deal in the vocabulary of the "real" New Haven.

The Dixwell Fire Station is a *celebration* of the traditional dullness of municipal architecture, which by being celebrated is somehow no longer dull in any pejorative sense.

The interiors of Venturi and Rauch's building, especially, borrow some 1950s, late Art Deco qualities. The flatness of the exterior, on the other hand, and its wonderfully intense saturated red color, looking as it does almost painted on the brick, are reminiscent of a neighboring church, the United House of Prayer for All People. The use of a buff brick wainscot at the garage doors appears to be another specific quotation from nearby auto repair shops; its context is changed, however, by putting the lighter of the two colors illogically on the bottom.

It is the *over-all* image of the building, however, in relation to its time and place, that seems particularly well chosen. The earlier Venturi and Rauch firehouse in Columbus, Indiana, reflects in its form a different program, but also represents the desire for a strongly graphic, Pop image. The Dixwell Fire Station—although it uses a kind of brick billboard as its main "architectural feature"—rejects specifically Pop devices because of the nature of New Haven. That is, there is a perception that in a place where every architect has an angle, the most impact is made by playing it straight. The impact of straight but intense and highly selective *reportage,* seen in the work of the photorealist painters and of recent photographers who employ similar methods, represents a natural outgrowth of Pop to which this building clearly owes a great deal. This is, then, a photorealist building, very much of its time and thus not entirely escaping New Haven's insistence on fashion. It is also, however, a real building (a super-real building), among the first architect-designed buildings in New Haven that can make that claim. It is hoped that there will be, by Venturi and Rauch and others, many more.

The carefully maintained, like-new look of the interiors is striking in combination with the like-old look of the finishes, which recall a standard institutional interior of the 1950s: light green glazed wall tile, marbleized floor tile in a checkerboard pattern, rubber cove bases and natural, colored aluminum hardware. Within this vocabulary there are small but noticeable shifts from the ordinary, combined with unusual precision in detail.

DIXWELL FIRE STATION, New Haven, Connecticut. Architects: *Venturi and Rauch—Robert Venturi, John Rauch, Arthur Jones, Leslie DeLong, Robert Renfro.* Engineers: *The Keast and Hood Company* (structural); *Vinokur-Pace Engineering Services, Inc.* (mechanical/electrical). Consultants: *Dian Boone* (interiors); *William Gennetti* (cost). Contractor: *J. H. Hogan.*

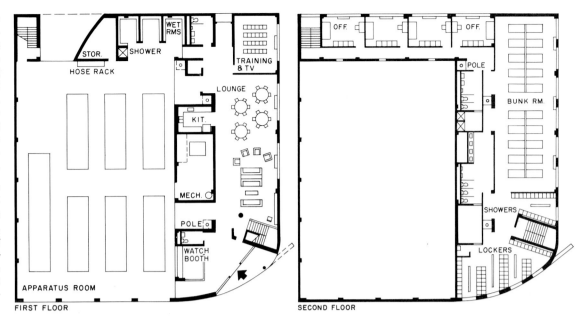

Cervin Robinson photos

For a sprawling urban renewal site in New Haven's Dixwell neighborhood, Venturi and Rauch were asked to plan a home for three formerly separate fire companies and a rescue unit. The result is a box within a box—the smaller one being a two-story "apparatus room" for fire engines and other equipment, and the larger one the almost-square building itself, which contains the apparatus room and everything else.

The big doors face neither of the two intersecting streets, but open instead onto the angled lane that connects them. This arrangement, and a wide apron, assures optimum maneuverability for trucks headed in either direction. It also assures, however, that the building does not face the major street (Goffe Street in the adjacent site plan). Thus the building is truncated on the Goffe Street corner to provide a pedestrian entrance.

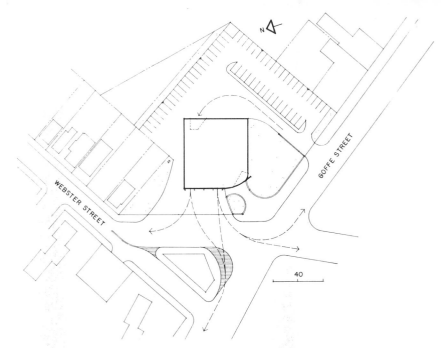

Above the entrance a brick wall that carries a long list of company names sails out into space. Most of the building is finished in a dense, but unglazed, brick with matching mortar; it produces a heightened version of common brick red, saturated enough to recall "fire engine red" in a city whose fire engines are white. Standard, natural finish aluminum windows and storefront glazing are used. But there are also special elements, in addition to the brick sign, to identify this as a public building: a flagpole set in a tiny but lush green lawn, and a small white marble veneer wall that marks the pedestrian entrance.

Venturi and Rauch photos

NEW
HARMONY
INN

Evans Woollen describes his firm's design for the new New Harmony Inn in New Harmony, Indiana, as "situational" architecture—an architecture that bends every effort to be particular to the place where it is built. In this case the place is a midwestern town of some 900 people, founded in 1814 by a communal sect of German Lutherans who called themselves Rappites. Ten years after the founding, the Rappites, having erected buildings in the manner of the men's dormitory shown in the small photograph on the following page, sold the town outright to Robert Owen, a wealthy cotton mill owner in Scotland, and they moved away. Owen hoped to found a utopian society based on universal education, and, though the communal aspect of his experiment was finally a failure, New Harmony survived as an important intellectual center well into the late nineteenth century. Later, at the instigation of the wife of a descendant of Robert Owen and of architectural historian Ralph G. Schwarz, New Harmony became the subject of renewed development to turn it into an important center for tourism and educational programs (without, it was hoped, the chaotic consequences that sometimes attend such endeavors). The 45-room inn is a major part of this refurbishing. According to Woollen, the first design, 12 years ago, for a site just outside the town, was strongly neo-Corbusian. Though it was in the end not built because the land could not be acquired, it elicited strong reactions. "It had a lot of amenities," says Woollen, "but nothing to do with New Harmony; people thought

Balthazar Korab

something would be lost if it were built." The town itself has several strong and readily identifiable qualities. The older buildings are no more than three stories high, and the important ones are made of brick, while the less important ones are of wood. None of them, moreover, seem quite as memorable as the over-all *format* of the town, which is characterized by streets lined with beautiful old trees.

The new inn is designed modestly to reinforce the existing situation. "By virtue of its having been off the beaten track, there is a built-in respect for context in New Harmony," Woollen says. "People in the 1870s went right on building like they had in the 1840s; their own world was bigger and more real than the world outside. It was as though a bell jar had been put over the town—and with the inn we

did not want to let too much air in."

Thus Woollen Associates' design for the inn, because of its effort to be particular to New Harmony, stands in contrast to its designs for other projects, like the Pilot Center in Cincinnati or the Indiana University Arts Center. Some will also note that it stands in contrast to Philip Johnson's famous "roofless church," which is virtually next door to the

Original Rappite Dormitory; below, Inn and "roofless church"

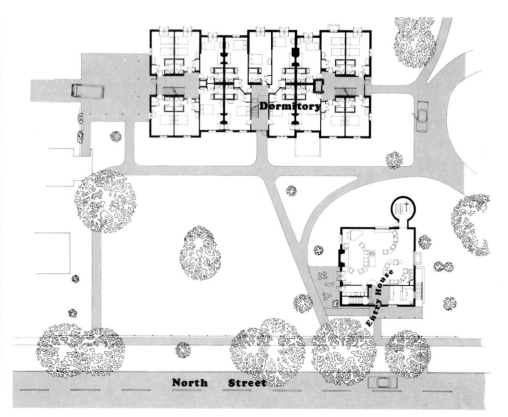

George Csema

inn and which can be seen in the lower left hand corner of the aerial photograph on page 151. (Recent reports indicate that the unfortunate deterioration of the church's ten-foot wall, and its consequent reduction in height by about half, have resulted in a happier scale relationship between it and the rest of the town.)

The New Harmony Inn consists of two separate buildings. The smaller one, and the one nearest the street, is the entry house, and it contains a registration area, a lobby and a small chapel in the rear. The lobby, which is shown in the photograph on the left, is large enough to encourage meetings, lectures and small concerts; and chairs, which are stored on the balcony level, can quickly be brought in for these purposes.

The larger building—or "dormitory" in allegiance to the lore of New Harmony—is organized not along long corridors, but according to the entry system, with rooms opening directly onto one of three stairways. One of the double-height suites on the third floor of the inn is shown in the photograph above.

Woollen Associates' design for the New Harmony Inn seems in every way "situational"—responsive to the context and the traditions of the place where it is built. But that raises a very important question: in being so modest, so particular to the place, is it being particular to *itself* (presuming, as architects usually do, that buildings are each meant in some way to be quite special)? Certainly no one would argue with the basic good sense of Woollen Associates' approach. But it is easy to

wonder whether their example will or should be followed by other talented professionals who will assist in New Harmony's current rejuvenation (including New York architect Richard Meier, who has been commissioned to design a new visitors' center). Whether or not the "situational" approach here satisfies everyone's expectations of what architecture should finally be, it seems eminently worth pointing out that that is certainly where it well must begin.

NEW HARMONY INN, New Harmony, Indiana. Architects: *Woollen Associates*. Engineers: *Robert Crooks* (structural); *D. A. Boyd Company* (mechanical and electrical). Consultant: *Kane and Carruth* (landscape). General contractor: *Chris Nix Company*.

George Cserna

The section on the right, taken through the Dormitory of the New Harmony Inn, shows a typical configuration of rooms and the way some rooms open on the back side of the building to terraces with a view of the nearby river. The photographs above and on the right show the straightforward and almost traditional style of the detailing and the furniture. The beds were designed by Woollen Associates; other furniture was obtained from domestic and Scandinavian manufacturers and chosen for its basic simplicity. The photo below, right shows the back of the inn.

George Cserna

Rustin Gesner

Balthazar Korab

NATHAN MARSH PUSEY LIBRARY

By partially burying this three-level library underground and covering its roof with grass, planting, and paths which reinforce the existing circulation patterns of Harvard Yard, architects Hugh Stubbins and Associates have added an essential structure while preserving open space. Glass windows, concealed by sloping berms along two sides of the exterior and a central light court introduce natural lighting to staff and reader areas. Shown above is the principal entrance. The mobile in black steel is Alexander Calder's "The Onion."

All the interiors and custom-built fixtures were designed by the architects. Nylon carpeting is used throughout except in bookstack areas. Most of the furniture is of oak, as is the trim. Walls are covered with a textured vinyl fabric with a flat off-white, non-reflective surface. The acoustic ceilings are also off-white. Chairs are upholstered in either muted tweeds or brown leather. The daylight is softened by window hangings of natural hemp in an open-weave geometric pattern. All metal, from the window mullions to the smallest door hinge, is of bronze or bronze-finished aluminum. Accent lighting is either incandescent, or fluorescent warmed by gold reflectors within the light fixtures.

The photo (top) is of the reading room for the theater collection. The principal corridor (middle) is an exhibition gallery. It contains four large oak framed, acrylic-fronted exhibition cases for changing exhibitions. The gallery opens into the lounge (left) with a long display case beneath the window overlooking the moat. The lounge is a hub that provides access to the theater collection and archives, as well as to the central circulation desk just visible at the edge of the picture.

This most recent addition to Harvard Yard is a courteous and restrained new library. It is a background building constructed for the most part below grade on a site that was too constricted for a building above ground. Harvard Yard, of course, is a place of great historic interest, a museum of nativee American architecture of every period and an environment ereveredby generations of Harvard students, Cambridge citizens, and lovers of campus architecture.

Before being asked to design the Pusey Library, Hugh Stubbins Associates had been engaged to survey the entire twenty two-acre Yard with the object of improving access and services.

After careful observation of the patterns of activity and circulation within the Yard, the architects proposed that it be completely closed to automobiles and parking except for service and emergency access. This was implemented by the university.

Originally it had been thought that the proposed library should be completely subterranean, but new concepts of landscaping led to the idea that the building could emerge at least slightly above ground. The architects foresaw an opportunity they have since effectively capitalized upon—that of designing the library in a way that would open up new vistas within the Yard as seen from the inside of the new structure, or from its landscaped roof. Just as importantly, allowing the building to surface brings daylight into the interiors.

From the beginning, the Pusey Library was seen as an interconnecting link among three existing libraries — Widener, Houghton and Lamont (see site plan right), and an extension of each. Its roof has become a link as well, its paths and landscaping reinforcing the existing circulation network in the Yard. Inside the library, the principal circulation corridor is directly beneath the main diagonal path on the roof. The three major entrances to the new library are at important campus nodes. The principal entrance is directly to the east of the grand staircase of the Widener Library; the second is at the corner formed by Houghton and Lamont; the third is adjacent to 17 Quincy, the former official residence of the president of the university, now used for miscellaneous functions.

The new structure, which has been so precisely and definitively attached to its neighboring build-

The view across the landscaped roof of the new library (right) is as seen from the front of the Widener Library. The steps lead to the principal diagonal path, which connects with the circulation system of the Yard. The main entrance of Pusey is below grade at the foot of a staircase to the right of this stair. The stairway (below) also leads to the landscaped roof of Pusey. It is located between Houghton Library and Lamont Library.

© Steve Rosenthal

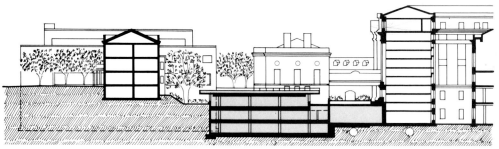
SECTION A-A

Edward Jacoby

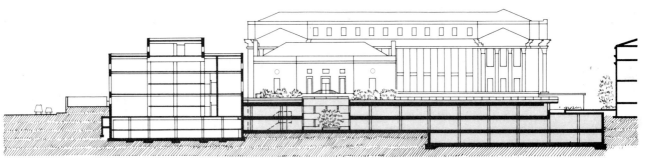

SECTION B-B

ings and to the campus infrastructure, adds 87,000 square feet to the buildings that comprise the Harvard College Library, which is a subdivision of the Harvard University Library, the largest university library in the world. Of the eight libraries within the College Library, three required their own reading rooms and better conservation of their priceless collections. These are the Harvard Theatre Collection, the Harvard University Archives and the Harvard Map Collection. The memorabilia of President Theodore Roosevelt needed adequate storage and display. Since, with the passage of time, books once regarded as commonplace have become rare, space had to be created that would allow such books to be kept at a temperature and humidity protective of their paper and bindings. Finally, as in all college libraries, the variety of services had increased and the collections were growing at rapidly accelerating rates. The new library accommodates the expanding general collections of Widener Library and the manuscript collections of Houghton.

In visible exterior form, the Pusey Library is a slanting grass-covered embankment as can be seen in the photos at right. Its roof is a stone-rimmed platform of earth containing a lawn, trees and shrubs, diagonally bisected by paths and stairs. On axis with the Neo-Georgian bow-front of Houghton is a square sunken courtyard (opposite page bottom right), which admits light to major interior spaces.

The portion of the building that appears above the surface is surrounded by a broad band of brick paving, which forms a moat between the berm and the window wall. At the top of the berm is a deep concrete trough planted with shrubs and vines.

NATHAN MARSH PUSEY LIBRARY, Harvard Yard, Cambridge, Massachusetts. Owner: *President and Fellows of Harvard College.* Architects: *Hugh Stubbins and Associates, Inc.—design: Hugh Stubbins, Peter Woytuk; project architect: Merle T. Westlake; project manager: Howard Goldstein; landscape: Robert Fager; interior design: Tetsuo Takayanagi.* Engineers: *LeMessurier Associates/SCI* (structural); *Haley and Aldrich* (foundations); *van Zelm, Heywood and Shadford* (mechanical/electrical). General contractor: *The Volpe Construction Co., Inc.*

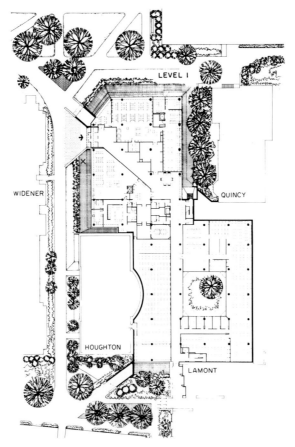

LEVEL 1

WIDENER

QUINCY

HOUGHTON

LAMONT

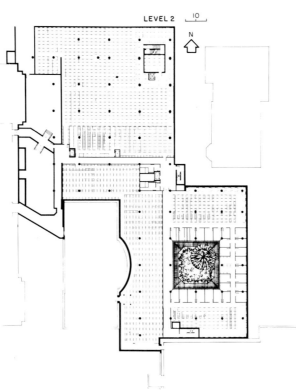

LEVEL 2   10

N

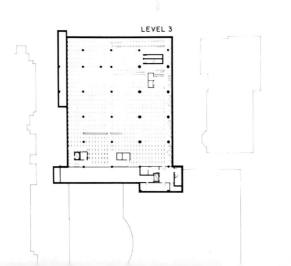

LEVEL 3

Edward Jacoby

Edward Jacoby

As the main level plan (opposite page top) indicates, the library has been organized to provide good visual control from the circulation desk located just beyond the lounge adjacent to the exhibition gallery. The photograph (top) shows the degree to which the apparent bulk of the library has been minimized by the slanting berm. To the left of the photo is the corner of Emerson Hall and 17 Quincy. To the rear are Lamont and Houghton and to the right is Widener. The courtyard (right) is two levels deep. It is faced with panels of shipsaw granite alternating with bands of glass. The court is a small garden with a brick surround.

Ronald Thomas, Attic & Cellar Studios, photos

1055 THOMAS JEFFERSON STREET

From John Adams to Jimmy Carter, people have come and gone for years, which is what Washington, D.C. is all about. But in its sedate, historic Georgetown district, even with moving vans lining the streets these days, there is a sense that people come and go less. There is, in fact, a feeling of status, and status quo, resplendently housed behind facades of brick, rigidly protected by rules of zoning, righteously observed by keepers of respectability. Little wonder, then, that new neighbors are given the cold shoulder until, by some mishap of etiquette, their habits are shown to be of heirloom civility. This has turned out to be the case at 1055 Thomas Jefferson Street (above, overleaf). A couple blocks from the Potomac River, 1055 is alongside the old Chesapeake & Ohio Canal, and, since it is there, Georgetown's keepers were especially concerned about architectural affrontery. So was the Washington Fine Arts Commission, which is empowered to keep rubes out of town and to avoid embarrassing environmental scenes. They need not have worried. Because the new building in town, even for the most suspicious, is fitting in very well, offering a spritely mix of activities, going about its business in a polite, pleasant fashion, and (the real test) showing respect for its elders. Designed by The ELS Design Group and Arthur Cotton Moore Associates, the new neighbor on Thomas Jefferson Street has not only accommodated the history of Georgetown, it is making some.

The main thing that is noticeable about the architecture of 1055 Thomas Jefferson is the spontaneity of public experience that occurs because of it. The clean lines and subtle scale of the six-story office building border and embellish the activities of the outdoor canalside "room" without overwhelming the environment. The ground floor, jutting out and back again, toward the refurbished Foundry, helps define this space full of amenity. The pitched roof of the Foundry deflects attention to the jutting lower floors and stepped-back terraces of the office building.

163

The story of 1055 Thomas Jefferson Street is a design and development story. Its structure is, more than brick-clad concrete, that of careful compromise. Its configuration is—beyond the skillful splicing of an historic environment with a lively interior mall, lined with 50,000 square feet of shops on two levels—a linking of community sentiments and physical context that have both been thoughtfully reflected. Its massing, stepped up from the side of the old C & O Canal in a series of terraced floors, expresses both conceptual discipline and legal constraint. It is a story of strategy, steeped in realities of the marketplace; in knowing that everyday people vote for, or vote against, buildings with their bucks. 1055 has turned out to be a very convenient polling place, and a very popular one, as well.

In Georgetown, whose citizens have been known to castigate developers with all the subtlety of Salem's attitude toward witches, the fact that people are coming around to like, use, and lease space in 1055 is telling testimony that an economically successful trade-off can be worked out between the keepers of history and the reapers of profit.

The mediators in this touchy situation, going back to 1970, were the architects—*two* firms of architects, in fact—The ELS Design Group (based in Berkeley and New York) and Arthur Cotton Moore Associates (based in Georgetown itself). It is unusual, to say the least, for a client to have two strong-willed, justifiably self-confident, design-oriented firms working *simultaneously* on a job. And it is even more unusual, under such circumstances, to end up with a building, especially one offering this much variety, that looks as though it was orchestrated by a single impresario.

This much variety? 1055 Thomas Jefferson orchestrates a lot. To begin with, it is popularly known as The Foundry, or The Foundry Mall. The reason is that the "cornerstone" of the complex *is* an old foundry, and it was determined, from the start, that it should be incorporated in the design as a way of smoothing the seam between the new construction and the older surrounding neighborhood. The Foundry, now a busy drinking and eating spot for swinging bureaucrats, and containing exhibits of the C & O Museum, was moved up the street about 100 feet. These interiors, designed by John Stulurow of California, are charming allusions to the past, but avoid cloying or corny effects. The Foundry Mall is a shop-lined two-level internalized "street" that threads through the new building at an angle, actually an enticing short-cut between the canalside and the Thomas Jefferson Street side, and this "street" is denoted by rows of exposed light bulbs. Its culmination is a two-level "piazza," and, in its center, there is a reflective pool with a generous stair poised above it. The stair angles down to the lower level at an intriguing jut of handrails and landings, providing impetus to go down and look. Edged by shop windows from every perspective, lined with wood signboards and recessed lights, the piazza gives the sensation of being *in* a shop

window. The Mall is as comfortable an experience as it is compelling, what with warm, tactile finishes of brick and wood, enhanced with crisp, reflective surfaces of metal and glass for the soffits and fascias. Feet move. Elbows rub. Eyes pop. Cash registers chime.

Rising above these two retail levels are five office floors. The over-all massing is adroit, as the terraced arrangement minimizes the sense of intrusiveness. The building's height is a third less than the permissible limit of 90 feet; yet five-sixths of the permissible density was achieved. Initially, yet another office floor was proposed, but in deference to the Fine Arts Commission, it was removed. Which is fortunate, because a subsequent zoning change requires one unit of floor-area ratio be given over to residential use, and a ratio of six applies here. Had that extra floor gone in, 1055 would now be a non-conforming building in a legal sense. Some floor-area allowance was picked up, anyway, by sinking the lower Mall level to the level of a basement thus deleting that square footage from the calculation. So the Fine Arts Commission and Georgetown got a lower building, certainly lower than was really necessary to satisfy environmental and historic considerations, and the client came fairly close to getting maximum density.

What one sees, sauntering along the bounding streets or the bordering C & O Canal is an architectural event, or, better, a well-coordinated set of events, that thoroughly embrace the location. Indeed, the Canal setting itself was approached as an integral element of the design. A park-like ambiance edges the opposite side, while 1055 edges its side of the Canal with a generous, landscaped esplanade, off from which are the entrances to both The Foundry and The Foundry Mall. The Mall provides a lively indoor space for the public—that "street" and "piazza"—and, because of its siting and massing, the new building, as a whole, defines a lively outdoor space for the public. The Mall is a room with a roof. The Canal and park create a room without a roof. Both must be counted as architecture—architecture as the courting of a public constituency, and as the countenance of human encounter.

The restored Foundry and the new building are carefully placed with respect to each other. The old element, in effect, anchors the new amidst the old. The lobby level nudges against it, its walls placed parallel to the Canal but set back a distance from it to create part of that outdoor room. The second floor, where the office spaces begin, is angled back from the roof of the lobby level, which thus gives a terrace. The second floor, in turn, gives a small terrace to the third floor. The third floor juts out toward the upper roof peak of The Foundry, and this jut gives yet another terrace up on the *fifth* floor. The intervening fourth floor and the top, or sixth, floor (both without terraces) give clear definition to the over-all mass, for all its angles and setbacks. The main mass of the building and the smaller jutting elements inter-

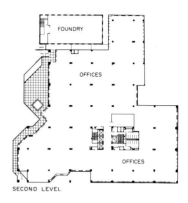

SECOND LEVEL

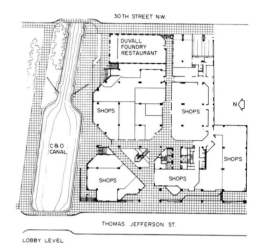

LOBBY LEVEL

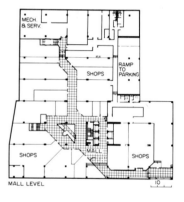

MALL LEVEL

Alongside the historic Chesapeake & Ohio Canal, the new construction, of subtle scale, stepped up to a height of six stories, skillfully spliced with the environment. This connection is enhanced by the incorporation of a 19th-century foundry (opposite, top) which was moved 100 feet to its present location and recycled for use as a restaurant and as exhibition space for the C & O Museum. The relationship of the old element and the larger new massing creates a wide esplanade by the Canal. On Thomas Jefferson Street (opposite, bottom), a strong, reinforcing edge is given to the district, while framing the canalside public areas.

penetrate each other and create visual balance. It is a good example of how a work of architecture can stand out and not stand out, all at once. And it is a good example of how architecture can fulfill itself by calling as much attention to the character of its surrounding, making room for the spontaneity of people, as to itself. One is put in mind that "the show is not the show," as Emily Dickenson once said, "but they who go."

Understanding "they who go" is the name of the developmental game

And attracting people to "the sweaty brawl of the marketplace" was the name of the design game here. Are such pragmatics theoretically respectable, conceptually sound, in determining the course that a design shall take? Is the flux of life, the ways people bump into each other, meet, do their business—is this flux of moment to architecture? It may be *the* moment to be calculated. And this is where the mediator role of The ELS Design Group and of Arthur Cotton Moore Associates became so valuable.

The client and the structuring of those interests are essential to understanding how 1055 came about:

Inland Steel Development Corporation, back in 1970 anyway, was, like many such subsidiaries of major corporations, bent on bringing back urban America. Few, however, were showing such strong concern for the *qualitative* aspects of their objective. David Carly, then the head of ISDC, factored them into front-end decisions, insistently cross-referencing design quality with bottom-line considerations. ISDC began operating on the premises that design quality would not only make its buildings look and work better but, by attracting people, make its bottomlines look and work better. Carly had yet another (and broader) commitment, pulling people back into our forlorn downtowns.

Carly was also willing to give new designers a chance—especially architects who shared his sense of the future of our country's urban resources, his sense that spending strategies can be as creative as design strategies, and his sense (going all the way back to the ancient but pertinent notion of *civitas*) that people, brought close together with a mix of purposes, are what give life to cities. (The ubiquitous suburban shopping center had taught many lessons about the movement of people and the profitability of that movement.)

In 1969, Carly hit upon The ELS Design Group, then barely formed—its principals, Barry Elbasani, Donn Logan, Michael Severin, (Geoffrey Freeman, who runs the New York office, joined in 1972). Dropping by their Berkeley office for what turned out to be a long, free-wheeling exploration of ideas, the simpático was cinched by, of all things, Severin's big white rabbit which, as Carly was beginning to talk, hopped onto the table. "*That* is a white rabbit," said the man, with a mix of fatigue and frustration. "That *is* a white rabbit," said Barry Elbasani. There would be many more long, free-wheeling explorations in Berkeley.

In the summer of 1970 they got a chance

to work together. Inland Steel Development Corporation was contacted by Canal Square Associates in Georgetown; who had previously developed Canal Square (designed by Arthur Cotton Moore), a mesmerizing amalgam of shops and offices, arrayed around a courtyard in a recycled group of buildings. Would ISDC consider, they asked, co-developing 12 or so acres of property in an area of Georgetown which, compared to most areas of Georgetown, was pretty down in the dumps? (For example, the site on which 1055 Thomas Jefferson is now located was a sand and gravel plant.) Carly hired ELS and the Real Estate Research Corporation of Chicago to help determine the design and marketing feasibility of such a venture.

That September, ISDC purchased for $12,-573,000 seven of the 12 acres, consisting of five different parcels held by five different owners; and set up five different subsidiaries to handle them. Canal Square Associates became minority stockholders in all five, a relationship which lasted until the fall of 1975, when ISDC purchased all such stock and recast the subsidiaries into a single concern.

One of the fortuitous aspects of the arrangement with Canal Square associates was its relationship with architect Arthur Cotton Moore, who, like the ELS team already acquainted with the project, had shown with his earlier Canal Square sound urban instincts, a firm belief in the interplay of old and new, culture and cash, and an *agora*-like meshing of places to buy things, learn things, or have fun.

By the fall of 1970, Inland was faced with a report full of facts about what the venture was going to entail; and, as any good developer knows, facts are what give you the rules to go by—certainly to *design* by. That's your "theory."

Here are some of the facts: Traffic had already become a nightmare in Georgetown; anything remotely resembling aggravation of the problem would surely result in resident shrieks and endless lawsuits. Such things that would also surely result were the new construction to clash—in its scale, massing, or finishes—with the surrounding area. The historic tone, texture of Georgetown was going to have to come out on top and no use in pretending otherwise, even if ISDC had *wanted* to pretend otherwise, which it didn't. Then there were technical problems, like how to build next to a canal or a river, with the structural precautions that had to be taken.

It was an unusual move, as mentioned before, but with all these facts before it ISDC (with Robert Larson as general manager of its subsidiary, Georgetown Inland Corporation) hired ELS *and* Arthur Cotton Moore—ELS, building upon their earlier feasibility studies for Carly, to do what one might call the bench mark work, basic urban design and architectural conceptualization; Moore, to carry on with design development, the refinement of structural features and spatial elements, and the final disposition of the key public areas. The contract, as unusual, called for routine consultation between the teams, in effect from

The lively spaces outside of 1055 Thomas Jefferson are interpreted inside as a sequence of "streets" leading to and around a two-level "piazza." Called the Foundry Mall, centered on a stair that is poised in the space above a pool and fountain, it is a specialty shopping center of 50,000 square feet, which has the spontaneity of a large family room. Warm, tactile surfaces of brick and wood, enlivened by transparent or reflective finishes of glass and metal, create an atmosphere that is compelling in a marketing sense and visually comfortable. A showcase for more than goods, the Foundry Mall shows that sociable, walkable scale is a successful marketing tool.

day one. So ELS sent its drawings to Moore, and Moore sent his drawings to ELS, as the schematic phase merged with the design development phase. Not surprisingly, both Elbasani and Moore, on separate occasions and 3,000 miles apart, have said, with something of a polite grimace, "It all became a blur."

An important tempering agent in this professional alloy was the firm of Sasaki Associates, retained about the same time for its urban-design insights and, later, to leaven those decisions with its landscape-design skills. Perhaps Inland was hedging its bets, but there is no doubt that Hideo Sasaki, a perceptive and persuasive critic, was an important factor in keeping the design, as it evolved, honest and open and clean. For his part, Moore also brought the indispensable presence and credibility of a Georgetown citizen to the job. There *was* resident resistance (and some lawsuits) but the Citizens Association *at least* regarded the Inland proposal as an estimable enemy.

One such lawsuit, alleging negative environmental impact, was won by Inland; yet another, still in process, alleges that the present mixed-use provision of zoning is illegal. This action pertains less to Foundry Mall than to further development, by Inland or anybody else, in the rest of the waterfront district. If won, it would tend to limit development to low-scale residential with a 40-foot height limit. This down-zoning would, one feels, be disastrous from the standpoint of sealing the waterfront area into a narrow eight-hour-day kind of mood rather than the otherwise vibrant round-the-clock complete environment already intimated by the qualities of 1055.

With architect Vlastimil Koubek brought on as associate to prepare construction documents and supervise the job, and with Tishman Construction brought on as construction manager, 1972 was the year that all of these facts, and conflicting facts at that, came together and the final set of design options was brought into focus. In April of 1972 ELS and Arthur Cotton Moore were released from their joint contract, and, like the couple of dozen other consultants on the job, were given separate ones.

It was at this point that the architects "ran for the daylight," as Vince Lombardi used to exhort his team. Considering the hot political environment, they ran toward what they considered to be the least offensive opening, choosing the present site over the four other parcels which ISDC had purchased in 1970. "Ideas in architecture," as Moore emphasizes, "are based on a tactical response to the realities that face you or square off to resist you. And these realities are not inherently evil, either. Here in Georgetown, it was a situation of carving out a potential within the political framework, a place where we could, in effect, try out certain concepts on a relatively small building, all the while studying these concepts for their implication at the larger scale." And Elbasani adds, "Pragmatic currents eddied about this job from the start, and you had to put in your stick to measure them. Putting in your stick to measure them, getting at the nature of the situation in which you are immers-

ing yourself, is 'master planning' in the *real* sense, not in the old out-dated illusory sense. You can't just ride into town anymore, like John Wayne, point at some prize, and say it's mine. They'll say, you can't have her. She's the sheriff's girl."

So although the architects' early strategy was to develop the entire five-parcel holding, they were, indeed, dealing with the sheriff's girl, and the site at 1055 presented a tactical, civilized way to get into town without the sheriff's calling out a posse.

In finally approving the design (the second time around), the Fine Arts Commission pointed out that it had turned out as good, if not better, than it would have had public sentiment had a formal input. The fact is that this sentiment *did* have an input because of the developers' and the architects' sound civic sense, and their understanding the realities of of the situation. The design strategy had been to propose a building that would seem, in Elbasani's words, "inevitably correct," which is a way of saying a building that would have a better chance of being realized. This inevitability, as a basic tactic and tenet of design, has made 1055 Thomas Jefferson an organic, orderly part of the Georgetown scene, and made people realize that new construction, stirring new uses in among what already exists, can reveal the scale, texture, and character of a community in a telling, enjoyable manner.

Last fall, with the shops of 1055 busy with Christmas buyers, people sitting in small groups along the Canal and enjoying the park, one of Georgetown's more sedate older citizens swallowed her pride and decided to take a walk toward the Potomac to see what, in fact, the new neighbor was like. "My God," she said, "this is the kind of thing I *wanted* here." With attitudes being recycled because of buildings like this, Georgetown may get more of what it wants, and, given as shrewd an architectural response, more of what it needs.

For Inland Steel Development Corporation, which, like many in the business these days, is laying low, keeping watch, there are signs of relief along with signs of elation. Paul Upchurch, who became general manager of the Georgetown effort in 1974 says, "We started out to prove, and we are proving, that excellent architectural design and careful consideration of the environment are basic to a fair return. After only a few months, the building, with all that had been going on around it and in it, *looked* like it had already been in Georgetown quite a while. I would say that is a very fair return, to everyone."

1055 THOMAS JEFFERSON STREET, Georgetown, Washington, D.C. Owner: *Inland Steel Development Corporation*. Architects: *The ELS Design Group* and *Arthur Cotton Moore Associates*. Associate architect: *Vlastimil Koubek* (construction documents and supervision). Consultants: *Sasaki, Dawson, and DeMay Associates* (urban design and landscape design); *Barton-Aschman Associates* (traffic and parking); *Arent, Fox, Kintner, Plotkin & Kahn* (legal); *Tishman Realty and Construction Co.* (construction management). General contractor: *Tishman Realty and Construction*.

© by Morley Baer

BILOXI LIBRARY
AND CULTURAL CENTER

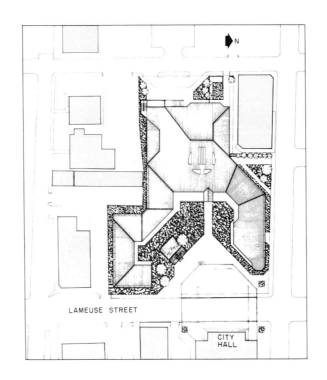

In May, 1975, teams of students from six Southern architecture schools, led by six nationally known architects, camped out for a week in Biloxi, Mississippi, to develop a series of alternative designs for the new library and cultural center which the town was then proposing. One of the team leaders, William Turnbull, of MLTW/Turnbull Associates in San Francisco, subsequently received the commission for the building, and now the job is done. The Biloxi library and cultural center is a centerpiece for a plan for what is hoped will be a comprehensive downtown renewal. Turnbull's building sprouts a pair of wings which embrace a newly created courtyard—originally conceived of as Biloxi's bicentennial gesture—where the town's original wood-frame library has been spruced up and relocated. The courtyard—which Turnbull calls a walled garden (a term whose meaning will be clearer once the space has been softened by the plants which have been placed there and once its live oak trees have had the chance to flourish)—

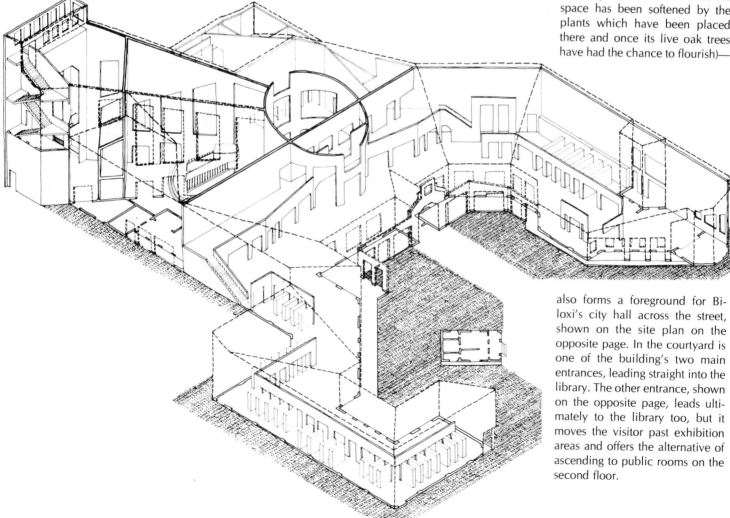

also forms a foreground for Biloxi's city hall across the street, shown on the site plan on the opposite page. In the courtyard is one of the building's two main entrances, leading straight into the library. The other entrance, shown on the opposite page, leads ultimately to the library too, but it moves the visitor past exhibition areas and offers the alternative of ascending to public rooms on the second floor.

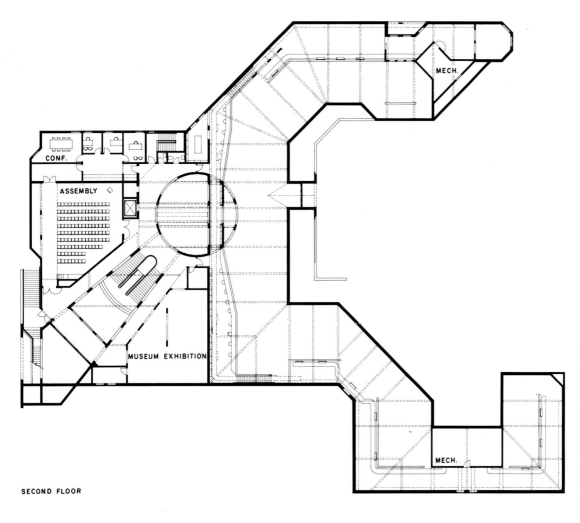

SECOND FLOOR

Some critics have dubbed the new Biloxi library and cultural center "Faculty Club South," a reference to the well known faculty club building which Turnbull and his partner Charles Moore designed for the University of California at Santa Barbara in the early 1960s. The collection of shapes and the look of the materials in the newer building help recall the older one, and here as well an irregularly composed plan is covered over with a relatively simple set of roofs which drape like a giant tent over the complexities which lie beneath. Layers of partly pierced walls, both inside and out, also help complete the stylistic picture. But the over-all effect is somehow sharper and clearer: a relatively simple program organized in an extremely straightforward way. Near the center of the building is a two-story circular space. The library is to one side, stretching itself around the courtyard outdoors. On the other side are administrative, service, and display areas. Two traffic systems reach into the center, and one of them does triple duty by serving the spaces on the second floor and by also becoming a memorable space in its own right. Gone, though, are the jarring and shocking cacophonies of the faculty club, replaced by something calmer. Gone, too, are the outrageous pieces of decor, since boars' heads and neon banners have now vanished in favor of simple wing chairs beneath a powder blue ceiling, serving more gently the functions of recall. Fans of the earlier building will no doubt detect a loss; others will detect something quite else—an altogether different kind of building.

BILOXI LIBRARY AND CULTURAL CENTER, Biloxi, Mississippi. Architects: *MLTW/Turnbull Associates*—*principal in charge of design: William Turnbull; project architect: Karg G. Smith.* Associated architects: *TAG, The Architects Group.* Engineers: *Rutherford and Chekene* (structural); *Marion-Cerbatos and Tomasi* (mechanical/electrical). Consultants: *Mississippi Library Commission* (technical consultant and purchasing for interiors); *Richard C. Peters* (lighting); *Paul Oppenheim* (cost). General contractor: *Holiday Inns, Inc., Construction Division.*
BILOXI BICENTENNIAL PLAZA, Biloxi, Mississippi. Architects for design: *MLTW/Turnbull Associates.* Construction documents: *Fairley Engineering.* Architects for the Old Creole Library: *Nicholas H. Holmes, Jr.*

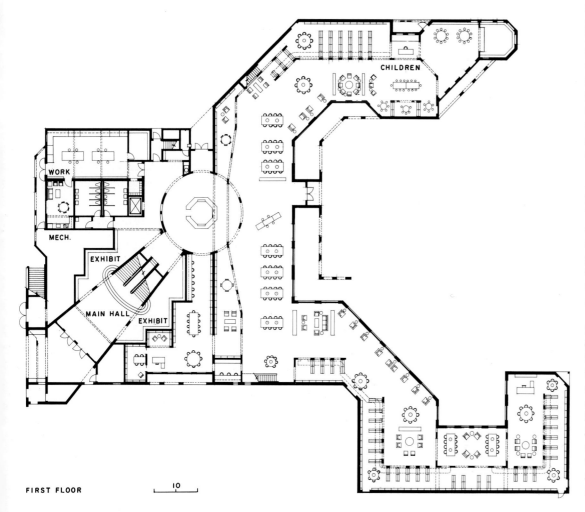

FIRST FLOOR   10

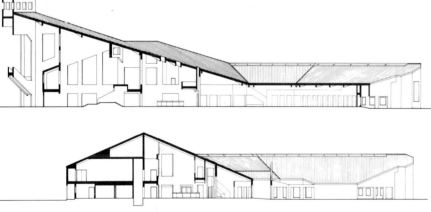

The photograph above shows the children's section of the library of the Biloxi Library and Cultural Center. On the right large windows face the courtyard. The photograph below shows the reading areas provided underneath the gently sloping roof on the upper level of the central part of the library, with the bridge that runs through the two-story circular space in the background. On the left are two sections taken through the building.

Index

DUE